CLAIM YOUR VOICE

*How to write the book that
only you can write*

FEN DRUADÌN

Forest Dragon Press

Published by Forest Dragon Press
Asheville, NC 28801, U.S.
Copyright © 2024 by Fen Druadin
All rights reserved.
ISBN XXX

Hard times are coming, when we'll be wanting the voices of writers who can see alternatives to how we live now, can see through our fear-stricken society and its obsessive technologies to other ways of being, and even imagine real grounds for hope. We'll need writers who can remember freedom–poets, visionaries–realists of a larger reality.

~ Ursula K. Le Guin

For Ken: Because you believed in me
For You: Because I believe in you

Table of Contents

INTRODUCTION:

CLAIM YOUR VOICE
What it means and why it matters

You have a book inside you. Or, perhaps you do. Or, you'd like to think that you do. Or, someone has told you that you do. And you've decided to pick up a book on how to make that possibility into reality. Congratulations, you are already one step closer than most people ever get to writing the book that only you can write.

One step closer to fully claiming your unique, authentic, powerful voice.

In these pages, I have condensed for you everything I have learned in my more than three decades of work as a writer, author, book coach, and developmental editor. I've organized and arranged it to help you get from where you are, to where you want to be: Holding a completed manuscript in your hands, ready for publication.

There are many wonderful books in the world that will help you in your writing journey. What this book does particularly well is walk you through the HOW to do it. Step by step, I'll guide you from "I have an idea (too many ideas, actually)" to "this is the book I always wanted to write, it's complete, and I'm proud of it."

We'll start with some high-level concepts and inspiration to get you oriented and pointed in the right direction. Then we'll get right into the nitty-gritty, step-by-step work of finally, actually getting it done.

So. Shall we begin?

Why Claim Your Voice?

The world is flooded with content: Massive quantities of automated spam and AI-generated drivel, alongside a good number of actually excellent books and resources. In such an environment, it's easy to wonder what purpose yet another book could possibly serve.

What can you say that hasn't already been said? How can you be heard through the ceaseless, grinding clamor of AI and cheap labor and everyone shouting from virtual rooftops?

And does it even matter?

One night, nearly three years ago, I lay under a starry sky on my sacred land and I asked this very question: How can I possibly make a difference? How can it possibly matter?

And the stars gave back an answer.

The answer is *your voice*.

You see, in all the world, there is no one exactly like you. There is no one who has lived what you have lived, no one who has done what you have done, no one who has seen the world through the precise lens of your point of view, and no one whose voice sounds exactly like yours.

And it is your authentic voice that the world is hungry for.

Tell me, when you read a book are you mining for information that you could find through an Internet search engine? Are you looking for the most recent generative AI summary of whatever topic the book is about?

Or are you looking for a journey with a brilliant mind whose company is worth your time?

There, under the stars, I saw it all laid out. We each have a part to play. We are like the mycorrhizal fungi among the roots of trees, seeking out connections, sharing resources, lighting each other up with each new thread we put out. And those who are called to write a book are called to a special purpose, the purpose of story sharing.

In all the human world, there is no force so powerful as that of a story to change hearts and minds, to nudge the human species toward something more beautiful, to create transformation at the deepest, biggest, and highest levels, to light up the night sky like the blaze of the milky way on a moonless night.

Isn't that a beautiful thought?

But nobody will hear your story if it is buried under layers of fear and insecurity and uncertainty. Nobody will hear your story if you try to hide it behind a facade of professionalism or perfection or excessive explanation.

You must unearth your authenticity, the spark that is uniquely yours, and allow it to shine through all the layers under which it has been buried.

To fulfill this vision, you must claim your voice.

What Does It Mean To Claim Your Voice?

And what does this mean, to claim your voice? First, there's finding it. Peeling back the layers of expectation to discover what's truly yours, who you are, what you sound like, how you speak to the world as your true self. Then, there's the courage to step into and claim your space in the world through that authentic voice.

That's what it means.

That's what I'm passionate about and what this book is designed to help you do.

Who This Book Is For

In my career, I have worked with individuals from all walks of life to help them claim their voice in many spheres:

Personally, professionally, in their social media presence, in their job searches, and through writing books, both fiction and nonfiction. I hope that anyone who wants to claim a more powerful presence in the world through their voice will find value here.

Almost anyone can use this as a guide to help them write the book they've always wanted to write. However, this volume is tailored especially to help purpose-driven individuals who want to multiply their impact by writing and publishing a nonfiction book.

Writing a book using the methods described here will help you strengthen the way you use your voice to communicate your ideas. It will clarify and amplify the way you influence and interact with others in your writing, and it will help you achieve more, both for yourself and for the world.

Why I Wrote This Book

This book is everything I know how to say, to help you claim your voice and birth your book, a book that will nudge the planet and transform your life. It is filled with the energy and insights of nearly five decades of reading, studying, and doing.

It contains Julia Cameron's *The Artist's Way*, which opened me up, and flayed me, like a patient etherized upon a table. It holds Anne Lamott's *Bird by Bird*, and Stephen

King's *On Writing*, and Anne Rice's videos for writers, and Ernest Hemingway's advice, and Robert McKee's incredible analysis of plot and character in *Story*, and Natalie Goldberg's *Writing Down the Bones*, and so many more (I contain multitudes).

It contains Whitman and Goodall and Dillard and Kimmerer. Jung and Shakespeare and Milton and Blake and Homer and Xenophon and Plato and Aristotle and Keats and Chaucer and all the introductions to dictionaries I read for fun in my father's library before I was fifteen (and so many more etymology and linguistics texts since).

It contains all the blogs I ever read about internet marketing and sales principles and the vicarious MBAs I earned through years of interviewing business owners, partners, and CEOs for business magazines. It contains my extensive experience in branding and messaging for new and existing products and companies. It contains all the classes I ever took in creative writing, marketing, and critical thinking.

It contains all the magic I ever studied, my mysticism and the arts I learned of effecting change without moving a finger, and the inside-out job of personal transformation. It includes my study of systems thinking and psychology, as well as biology and brain science.

It contains all the aborted attempts at stories and novels and books tucked into crevices all over my house, and the box of hand-illustrated stories I dreamed up as a child, the box that my mom keeps in her basement just in case I'm famous one day.

It contains everything I learned from working with dozens of authors to help them birth their books, and everything I've learned from birthing my own.

Nothing gives me more joy than helping authors go from "crying in their coffee" to producing a manuscript they're proud to share with the world. Watching them go from "I know I need to write this but I don't know where to begin" to booking signings and speaking engagements and celebrating a legacy they didn't know if they'd ever live to see.

My process, outlined in this book, is the mushroom arising from the soil of a lifetime of study and practice.

I know this process works.

And I know your book deserves to be born.

And so, I give you, from my hands to yours: This.

The reason I wrote this book?

Because I believe in the power of your voice to change the world.

I believe in you.

How to Use This Book

There are a hundred "how to write a book" books out there, and I'm honored for this one to take its place among them.

We all stand on the shoulders of giants, and I wouldn't have written this book if I weren't inspired by the dozens of others I've read.

I also wouldn't have written it if I didn't know that I have something to say that hasn't been said yet.

This book is intended to inspire, but it's also a very practical, very hands-on, how-to-do-it book that outlines a *proven* process that has helped hundreds of people like you to finally write the book that *only they can write*.

The book is divided into three main parts. The first part is designed to be worked through, workbook-style, before you begin writing your first draft. If you have already begun writing your book, that is not a problem. Take a pause and work through the exercises in the first part anyway. They will help you hone, refine, and clarify the work you are already doing, which will result in a stronger final manuscript.

The second part of the book is designed to help you make your way through the weedy, overgrown, twisting path to a first draft. It contains essential mindsets and information to help you get started, avoid common pitfalls, and recover when life throws you curveballs. It also contains a guided journey through Root 11, my proprietary (and extremely effective) tool for clearing writer's block. Even if you already have a first draft of your book, I recommend reading the Root 11 chapter (which is chapter 11!) because creative blocks can crop up at any point in the process.

Part three will guide you through the revision process after you have a first draft. Many people who have never written a book think that it's all just writing. But we who have done it know that revisions are actually the bigger part of the job. No matter where you are in the writing process, this section will help you choose the professionals who can help you best, navigate the difficult terrain of structuring and editing your draft, and produce a manuscript you'll be proud to call your own.

To get the most out of this book, I recommend taking a quick look at the table of contents to see the high-level topics contained inside. Then, even though it can feel like going backwards, start at the beginning. You can skip the middle section (but not chapter 11!) if you already have a draft, but don't skip the first part, no matter what. Use the table of contents to guide you if you want to skip around to the bits that are calling out to you, and follow your instincts. You already have everything you need inside you: Let this book help you to unlock it.

Now, Bring Us Your Voice

You are why I do the work I do.

I believe in the voices of real humans, with real solutions, with real ideas, with real visions.

You are not Mark Twain or Mary Shelley or J.R.R. Tolkien. You are not Daniel Pink or Seth Godin or Glennon Doyle. You are something better. You are yourself.

And nobody is better at being you than you. Nobody is more beautiful in the essential beingness of you than YOU.

Your audience, your people, your readers, your customers, the people you have the ability to impact: It's YOUR voice they want. It's YOUR voice that makes them listen. It's YOUR voice that carries them along on the journey you want to share with them.

So, let's do it. Let's bring the world your voice.

PART I

BEFORE YOU WRITE
What to do to secure your success

Authors often come to me mid-draft, feeling lost. They've already written thousands or even tens of thousands of words, but now they're stuck. They may think it's their busy life (which can be a factor) or their ADHD (could be) or a shameful lack of discipline (no, it's not that) that's getting in the way.

They may have read a lot of books and blogs about writing, know all the "right things" to do, and now blame themselves for still not being able to finish.

But the real reason most authors don't finish their books is that they weren't set up for success before they began. A lot of writing advice, in all the thousands of books and blogs about writing, amounts to: *Just write*.

Write that shitty first draft. Do it bit by bit. Unload yourself onto the page. Write it all in then take most of it out.

And don't get me wrong! This can all be great advice.

And for some authors, it is *enough*. These authors "just do it," and then they create a second draft and then a third and then a 52nd and then a "52nd FINAL FINAL THIS IS THE ONE REALLY THIS TIME OMG (17).docx" (iykyk) and eventually they declare themselves done and publish the thing.

Lucky ducks.

For the rest of us, that advice gets us started, full of vim and vigor, and gets us as far as a stack (or ten) of unfinished manuscripts, and another few stacks of shame and self-blame.

What authors need isn't more "just doing it." What we need are *tools*.

You wouldn't start building a cabin without bringing your blueprint and your toolbox. Nobody would tell you: "Just put in your time. Go out to the woods, look at other cabins, start building and don't stop till you have a cabin."

The same thing goes for reaching a distant destination. If you plan to complete a long journey through challenging territory where cell signal is absent and the route isn't marked, you won't just step out your front door and start walking till you get there. You need to know where you plan to end up, what direction to go, what kind of terrain you will be covering, the best route to take, any vehicles you'll need and how to operate them, where you can take rest stops, and what supplies will be necessary to keep you going. Your maps, supplies and equipment form a critical "toolbox" without which you will fail.

Writing a book is a long and challenging journey across uncertain terrain, with more than a few obstacles along the way. Give yourself the gift of the right toolbox to secure your success.

The Writer's Toolbox

Your Vision

Your North Star Statement

Understanding Narrative Structure

Your Outline

Your Writing Plan

Planned Rest Stops

Your Technology

Your Parking Lot

Is ADHD Stopping You From Writing Your Book?

Maybe. But it doesn't have to.

Almost everyone I work with is neurodivergent. Most authors I've ever met have some version of ADHD, autism, twice exceptionalism, high intelligence, "giftedness," or whatever the latest

---

neurodivergent diagnoses are, whether they've ever been diagnosed or not.

Weird, right?

But not really. Writing a book is not exactly a *normal* thing to do. It is, in and of itself, a divergent activity, in that it diverges from what most people do.

The brain that envisions a book is simply a different kind of brain from most. The drive to do something extraordinary is not separate from neuro-divergence. It is part of it.

The neurodivergent brain can make life hard. It may have a hard time focusing (there are so many things to think about! The world is full of fascinating distractions). It may cause us to hyperfocus (the brain is engaged and the endorphins are flowing, MUST KEEP GOING). It can lead to depression (all that sensory and intellectual input can be EXHAUSTING, not to mention the ostracism we experience and the struggle of realizing that the rest of the world doesn't see what we see) and anxiety (we see ALL the dangers and all the wide-ranging implications thereof).

The neurodivergent brain also tends to be dis-paraged and disabled by societal expectations and structures. In our current society, we lucky "neuros-picies" rarely survive childhood without significant trauma. Yippee! Add CPTSD to the mix.

But the neurodivergent brain is not an accident or flaw or a curse. It is a non-normative brain structure, but it is an intentional one, an emergent quality of the human species, and it is necessary to our survival and thriving as a species. The fact that we have pathologized it for most of written history does not alter the fact that it has also been the biggest source of adaptive change, creative expression, and valuable invention across that same history.

The neurodivergent brain is one that thinks deeply, widely, creatively, and systemically. It is a brain that makes connections and sees things that others don't see.

Properly supported and freed to do what it does best, the neurodivergent brain is a brain that will change the world. Our evolutionary purpose is to help our people break loose from structures that no longer serve us, and move into models of being that do.

We are the visionaries of our people, and our role is sacred, whether the world recognizes it or not.

For this reason, any book coach, developmental editor, or book about writing books must acknowledge and be ready to work with brains that don't submit to the standard ways of thinking and being. We must create structures that work *with* instead of against our native abilities.

Your ADHD or autism or giftedness or other brain differences may be stopping you from writing a book. But it doesn't have to.

Everything in this book is designed to serve the needs of the neurodivergent brain. The tools and techniques and approaches herein are field tested with real neurodivergent authors, time and time again, and shown to be effective in supporting the neurodivergent brain in finally actually finishing that book.

With that in mind, remember that divergent means *not the same*. So no matter how well-tailored this book is to neurodivergence (and it is), not everything will apply to you. Use that big connections-making brain to discern what applies and what doesn't, and at all times: Follow your own inner knowing.

CHAPTER ONE

YOUR VISION
illuminates your destination

If you wanted to travel to a distant and glorious destination, the first thing you would do is dream. Dream about where you will go and why and what you will do there. Dream about what the destination will look like and feel like, what amenities you will enjoy, and what activities you will engage in when you get there. A fireplace, a library, a deck, big windows. A rainforest, a beach, an ancient ruins. Hiking, dancing, studying, sightseeing.

You would dream that this vision might be possible for you, and you would follow your heart and your passion to make it happen just the way you want it.

That vision is what would carry you through the arduous journey of actually getting there.

The same is true for your book. Before you sit down to write, even before you start assembling the rest of your toolbox, you need a vision to carry you through. A vision may not always be tangible, and it may not seem practical, but it is the magic that makes everything else possible.

The good news is that the vision is already inside you.

The magic lives in your heart and mind.

The fact that you want to write a book, that you feel you have a gift the world might like to have, is evidence enough that you have what it takes to get there. Whatever it is that you are feeling the need to share, that's the magic, that's the vision.

So, first things first:

Trust it. Believe it. Before you write the first word on a page, know that your power is real. You can do this, and by picking up this book, you have already begun.

The journey will not be easy. If it were easy, everyone would write a book. After all, there are few vehicles more powerful for spreading our ideas and building a platform for our work than a book. Few better ways to establish our authority, to drive our dreams forward, to connect with the people we want to connect with.

If it were simple, and if the path were well-worn and swift, wouldn't everyone do it?

Along the way, you'll face many perils: Despair, imposter syndrome, fear, shame, the conviction that everything you write is garbage (even when it's not). The conviction that *you* are garbage. Sometimes just: Life, coming at you fast.

You will hit points where you don't know if you can continue. If it's even worth it.

But you can do this. I believe in you. And by the time you're done, you will believe in you too.

I have worked with people from all walks of life, from CEOs of hospital systems to attorneys and accountants, from burlesque dancers to spiritual leaders and single moms building a better world for their children. Every one of these people lives busy, full lives of career, family, hobbies, and avocations. Almost all of them are neurodivergent with brains and work patterns and lives different from all of the others. Every one of them found, with my assistance, a path through the book-writing wilderness that fit their life and their work style. It's hard, but when you have a clear vision and a good toolbox, you can do it too.

So, let's get started, shall we?

EXERCISE: DREAM THE DREAM

Estimated Time: 25-30 minutes

Find a safe and peaceful place to work. Make yourself a cup of tea or cozy up under a favorite lap blanket. Make yourself comfortable. Place a notebook and pen, or a laptop, or other recording device nearby.

Set a timer for twenty-five to thirty minutes, and allow yourself to stay within your dream space for at least that long. If you have time-sensitive obligations later in the day, set an alarm for them so that you are not worrying about whether you will forget them.

Set your intention: You are about to dream the biggest, brightest, most beautiful dreams for yourself and your book imaginable.

Now, allow yourself to breathe. Take several deep breaths and focus on the air going in and out of your lungs. Allow your muscles to relax. Allow your mind to wander without forcing it to comply. Feel yourself settling into a space where anything–anything at all–is possible.

In this space of infinite possibilities, ask yourself:

- If anything were possible, what would you dream into existence?
- If anything were possible for you, what would you ask for?

- If anything were possible for your book, what would you want it to do?

Let your answers be exactly as big or as small as they want to be. Allow your mind to wander and dream big dreams, no matter how impossible they may seem. Or wander and dream small, cozy dreams that feel delicious to you.

Allow yourself to feel into a space where what matters is what feels good to you, what feels right inside your body.

One of the authors I worked with dreams of a world in which wealth is measured by the health of our ecosystems. Another dreams of one in which women claim their power through owning their bodies. Yet another wants to see men reclaiming their health and balance in mid-life. New banking systems, stronger international cybersecurity, more personal freedom: These are all dreams authors have dreamed in sessions with me. One author simply wants her daughter to understand how much she loves her.

Your dreams are yours, and can be whatever you want them to be. Take your time with this. Then, when it feels right to you, write down what you've dreamed, or record it with your voice.

This is your vision. Hold on to it.

CHAPTER TWO:

YOUR NORTH STAR STATEMENT
clarifies your direction

You have dreams, and dreams can be immeasurably valuable. But they are only clouds in the sky unless you know how to reach them.

In fact, big dreams can be demotivating rather than motivating when they feel unachievable. So the next thing we are going to do is create clarity and focus, an achievable yet inspiring destination to point toward, and the direction to go.

This we will do with your North Star Statement.

Your personal North Star is where your heart points you most strongly. It is a magnetic pull toward what you came into this incarnation to do. You have found your North Star when you know exactly what direction you want to go, even if you don't know what the journey will require of you.

Your North Star for a book is the same thing, aligned with your personal North Star, yet specific and detailed enough to pull you like a magnet attracting the point of a needle, toward the completion of your book. Your North Star Statement consists of a clear and motivating understanding of who you are writing for, what this book will be about, and why you are writing it.

Like many authors, Deann, a mental health expert, wanted to create big changes in the world, and she had a million ideas and stories swirling around in her head, but no idea where to begin. When Malcolm, a hospital CEO, realized it was time to write his book, he knew he wanted to share the many stories of his forty-plus-years of adventure and accomplishment. He had the commitment, the history of achievement, and the work ethic to do it. What he didn't have was clarity around where to begin. Julie, a print shop owner, knew she wanted to tell the story that her mother couldn't tell, the one that would help other women free themselves from the cages that once held her, but the project felt overwhelming.

All three of these authors came to a workshop with me and answered a series of questions, brain dumped their thoughts and ideas into the sacred space I held and, at the end of the workshop, stepped through a portal into a world where they knew exactly what they must do. And they did it.

That workshop is the one I now deliver as my North Star Workshop, and I am going to share its secrets here with you. The success metric for the North Star Workshop is an "aha" moment. Sometimes this shows up as a deep breath. Sometimes as chills. Sometimes it shows up as a smile or even tears (I love tears). However it shows up, I know we've found the North Star the author needs only because *they* know they've achieved it.

The deliverable from the workshop is a single sentence that brings together everything the author needs in order to begin with confidence and clarity:

- What the book will be about
- Who you are writing for
- And, importantly, WHY you are writing it

The right North Star Statement will leave your fingers tingling, itching to get started. It will pull you through even the toughest moments of your writing journey. Here's how to manifest the North Star Statement that will pull you in the direction you want to go throughout the journey of writing your book.

"Without Fen... I would still be crying in my coffee."
Janet Barrett,
Author of *Stop The Break*

EXERCISE: MANIFEST YOUR NORTH STAR STATEMENT

Estimated Time: 90-120 minutes

For this exercise, you will need to set aside at least 90 minutes. Two hours is better. Provide yourself with the note-taking tool(s) you prefer (pen and paper, computer, or a voice recorder with transcription software are all reasonable choices), and a non-alcoholic beverage of your choice. Make sure you are in a safe and protected space, and that you are unlikely to be disturbed. The mindset for most of this exercise is one of creativity and open flow, so try not to limit yourself.

Then follow the steps below.

Step One: Name Your Why

Understanding your deep inner "why" is the key to sticking with any major task. If it seems pointless, you won't do it. But if you know why you're doing it and that "why" is hot and juicy and wildly compelling, then you will. It really can be as simple as that.

So let's find and name the hot, juicy, wildly compelling "why" that will compel you to write the book, shall we?

The "why" for any book consists of two key components:

1. The changes you want to see in the world as a result of your book

2. The changes you want to see in your life as a result of the book

Take a few minutes to review the notes you made in last chapter's Dream the Dream exercise. Breathe deeply, and open your heart to allow more specific dreaming as we move into the nitty gritty of this exercise.

With the device of your choice, you will record your answers to the following questions. Don't censor yourself or try to make it make sense just yet. Just record whatever comes to mind for you. If you're using a voice recorder, make sure you have transcription software running in real time, so you can review the notes for later steps in this process.

You don't have to answer the questions in order. It's okay to jump around, or even to skip some questions. Use them as a launching point to think in more detail about what you want.

1. What are your dreams and goals for yourself and, if applicable, your business this year?
2. What about in the next five to ten years?
3. Imagine your book is complete and published, and it's out in the world making a difference. Imagine that it is doing everything you could possibly hope that it might do. How is the world different because of it?

4. Imagine the same thing, but now take the focus and put it on yourself. How is your life different?

5. How does what you are imagining line up with the dreams and goals you listed at the beginning? How does it not align with them?

6. Why have you chosen to invest your time, energy, and money into this book project?

As you do this work and review your answers, what patterns emerge for you? What aspects of your hopes and dreams have been revealed? What aspects have been clarified and strengthened? Did anything surprise you?

Did anything light you up inside like a match to kindling? Take note of that.

Make a few summary notes about what is standing out to you the most, especially what feels "hot" and important.

Then hold onto your thoughts. We will come back to this in the last step.

Step Two: Clarify Your Who

Which is easier, to write a book or to talk to a friend? One of the foundational mindsets for writing your book is the understanding that, in the end, every great book is just a conversation with a friend.

That doesn't mean the book won't speak to hundreds or thousands or maybe even millions of people. It only means that as each person reads it, they feel as though

"In the end, every great book is just a conversation with a friend."

you are speaking to them specifically, directly, as a friend. And in order for your book to do that, you need a clear idea of who that friend is.

The "friend" you are looking for is the person you most want to reach with your book.

One concern many authors have at this point is that they don't want to limit themselves to a narrow audience. Don't worry. You don't have to exclude anyone. We're not going to prevent you from reaching everyone if everyone wants your book.

What we are trying to do is establish the readers who will be *most* attracted to and impacted by your work, the people you can help the most. When you narrow your focus to those people, you'll be more focused in your writing and, counterintuitively, your writing will end up appealing to a wider audience because you narrowed your focus.

Ready? Just as in the first step, you're going to use your recording device and an open, calm mind to answer these questions in any order that appeals to you.

- Who do you *want* to write for?
- When you think of someone picking up your book and becoming absolutely engrossed by it, who do you imagine?
- Describe them in detail.
  - What are they wearing, what kind of job do they have, what characteristics do they exhibit (gender, race, national origin, religion, age, marital status, LGBTQ+ status, disability, geographic location, and so on)? Are they rich or poor or middle class?
- Think about where they are in life right now and write about that. Are they stuck in a dead-end job or excited about a new chapter in their life? Has something stressful just happened or are they planning their next vacation? Are they excited, fearful, celebratory, anxious? Try to come up with as much detail as you can.
- Who *needs* this book? Are they the same person you just described, or someone else? How are they different?
- Who can you help the most? Is this the same as you've already described? Are there additional characteristics, differences, or new important factors?
- How are the three people described above similar? What do they share in common?

- What pains are they feeling that your book can help alleviate?
- What aspirations are they striving toward that your book can help them achieve?

When you feel complete, briefly review what you've written. Highlight or circle portions that stand out for you. Then move on to step three.

Step Three: Define Your What

Once you know why you are writing and who you are writing for, your "what" can emerge. With your "who" in mind, explore and record your answers to these next questions, in any order.

- What problems can your book help your "who" solve?
- What results can you promise them?
- What book does your "who" *want* to read? See if you can picture it in your imagination.
    - What does it look and feel like?
    - How thick is it?
    - How heavy?
    - Is it full of words or images or graphs?
    - Is the cover soft or hard?

- Does it contain exercises and reflections, stories and essays, hard-hitting facts and statistics, deep insights, practical how-tos?
- What would make the person described in your "who" pick it up off a bookstore shelf and think, "Oh, I need this book!"?
- When your reader is done with your book, what do you hope they will take away from it?

When you've spent some time on this, review your notes. As with the other steps, highlight anything that stands out for you.

Step Four: Write Your North Star Statement

Now the magic happens. We're going to take these pages and pages of notes and condense them down into a single, clear statement that will serve as your North Star throughout the writing process.

But before we do, it's important to take a moment and become clear about what a North Star Statement is not.

- It is not a book blurb or an advertisement. You're not trying to sell the book. You're trying to get clear about why you're writing it, for whom, and what it's about.

- It is not for anyone but you. Don't worry about whether it will appeal to anyone else or even whether it will make sense to them.
- It is not short and punchy and perfectly grammatical (unless you want it to be). We're going for accuracy and clarity, not brevity.

You will know you have gotten your North Star Statement right when you read through it and feel a sense of clarity. You may also feel relief, joy, excitement, warmth, motivation, or even tears. This is the "aha!" moment I mentioned earlier.

To get there, you're going to take everything you've done in the previous steps, and fit it into a very specific structure, like a Mad Libs for grown-ups. Here's your format:

I will use my book to [help, inspire, attract, or other verb] [who] by [teaching, showing, helping, inspiring, or other -ing word] them [what], which will lead to [why].

Pay special attention to the areas in your notes that you have highlighted when defining your who, what, and why for the statement. It's okay if it gets wordy, but try to contain each portion to about three key elements.

To get you started, take a look at these real client examples:

"I will use my book to empower sellers who are hungry to grow and win, by teaching them to avoid commoditization, ask the right strategic questions, recognize the signs when the sale is at risk of getting derailed and keep it on the rails, which will lead to my big why to celebrate, defend, and uplift the sales profession."

(Jennica Dixon, *Wimp Junction*)

"I will use my book to inspire and incubate people (especially women) who feel miscast in their life and afraid to break out of the box or go off-script, by instilling urgency and teaching them how to strip down, occupy their body, and claim themselves, which will lead to my ultimate goal of helping open doors within and for people to live out loud."

(Shannon Varner Alexander, *Bonnie Bodacious*)

"I will use my book as a bridge, to help high level executives and their cybersecurity teams see and understand themselves in new ways, by introducing concepts, building bridges, and experimenting with approaches, which will lead to my 'big why' of nudging the universe in a positive way."

(Chris Brown, *The CISO Secret*)

"I will use my book to help dreamers, visionaries, and weirdos like me birth the books they want to birth, by showing them both the nuts and bolts and the emotional and spiritual aspects of getting from an idea to a completed manuscript, which will lead to my ultimate goal of more people claiming their power and their voice."

(Fen Druadìn, *Claim Your Voice*)

As you can see, one hallmark of a great North Star Statement is that it will not be exactly like any other North Star Statement in the universe. Each one is wildly unique and specific, even within the same basic structure. You'll also notice that most of them don't labor over being perfectly grammatically correct, and most of them are much longer than an ordinary sentence would be.

The goal is not to produce your most scintillating piece of copy, but rather to capture the heart and soul of what you are doing, in just a few lines of text. It's not an easy ask, but it's a worthwhile task.

Don't worry if it takes a while to get your aha moment. Play around with it. Keep going till it feels right.

When you get that moment of clarity, you won't believe how good it feels.

Step Five: Print It Out and Post It

When you feel good about your North Star Statement, it's time to make it real. And by real, I mean put it on paper.

Our brains (especially those belonging to we neurospicies) are good at focusing on what's right in front of us, and bad at remembering what's not. So put that statement right in front of you: On your desk, by your bed, on the refrigerator door. Some people like to make it the wallpaper on their primary writing device.

You want it to constantly remind you *that* you are working on a book, *why* you're working on it, *what* it's about, and *who* it's for. With that right in front of you every day, you will find it much easier and more motivating to put in the time to get it done.

And now it's time for a rest break. Throughout this book, you will periodically encounter the following graphic:

REST STOP

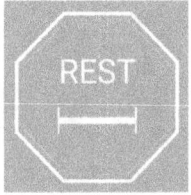

These are not randomly placed. They are a critically important part of the writing process, strategically inserted exactly where your brain needs them most. In chapter six, we'll explore why and how to approach your rest periods in more detail. For now, the main thing is, right now, as soon as you're done writing your North Star Statement: Take a break of at least one week before moving forward to the next step.

Note: You can always *read* ahead in this book, but don't *work* ahead on your book. Flip to chapter six for why.

CHAPTER THREE

NARRATIVE STRUCTURE
maps the terrain

With your North Star Statement in hand, you know the direction you're pointed in. Now I want to have a word with you about the terrain your reader will travel when your book is complete. In the book world, the "terrain" is called narrative structure. It's the ground you cover in the course of reading a book. And therefore, it's the terrain you will create as you write your book.

Understanding narrative structure is critical for developing your outline and for writing a book that has the impact it deserves.

A Lifetime of Narrative Study

It's no accident that my life's work is helping other people claim their voices and their stories. I was

---

reading before I could walk, and writing stories after school for fun for as long as I can remember. I read Shakespeare (*All's Well That Ends Well* to be precise) at age eleven and *War and Peace* at sixteen. I earned a bachelor's in English literature in 1995 and went on to study classics like Homer, Cicero, and Aeschylus in their original languages in grad school at the University of Iowa.

I've worked in branding, messaging, and storytelling for companies like Autodesk (where I helped them refine the story of their construction suite during its early days) and I've been Head of Storytelling for a Swedish software firm that supports sales organizations all over the world. I've helped countless start-ups nail their stories to support their brand. I've published several volumes of my own work, and won creative writing contests and industry content awards on behalf of clients. I maintain a heavy presence on Facebook where I channel stories from the natural world into inspiration and support for the human world.

I have lived and breathed narrative, and studied it professionally, my entire career. I have read all the major literature on the subject of writing and narrative. Aristotle's *Poetics* and Plato's *Republic*, Carl Jung's

The Structure of the Psyche and Robert McKee's *Story,* Stephen King's *On Writing* and Julia Cameron's *The Artist's Way.* Anne Lamott's *Bird by Bird* and Natalie Goldberg's *Writing Down the Bones* and on and on, not to mention watched hundreds of hours of YouTube videos and master classes from luminaries like Anne Rice and many whose names are less familiar.

In this next section, I condense all of that to the essentials you most need to know in order to write the book that only you can write, in the way that will reach the people you need to reach.

What Is Narrative Structure and What Is Narrative Arc?

"Narrative structure" is a fancy term for the order in which information is shared. Every book, story, blog post, and snippet of intelligible written or spoken content has narrative structure.

Narrative structure is how information is arranged. That's it.

Narrative structure can be good or bad, well executed or poorly managed. Great narrative structure will make your information clear, interesting, easy to absorb, and compelling to your reader.

Poor narrative structure will leave them bored, frustrated, and confused. A poor narrative structure will generally mean your readers don't finish or, even if they do, they don't get what you wanted them to get from it.

Narrative arc is one (extremely important) way to use narrative structure to get readers to want to consume that information. Narrative arc creates an emotional journey for your readers that keeps them listening, absorbing, and wanting more.

Narrative structure is the framework on which you build a narrative arc.

In simplest terms, narrative structure consists of a beginning, a middle, and an end, often with many smaller beginnings, middles, and ends within. A narrative arc occurs when you use the beginnings, middles, and ends to create an emotional journey for the reader. With a great narrative arc, you will leave the reader different than when they began.

"Narrative structure is how the information is arranged. Narrative arc is how you get readers to want to consume that information."

If you visualize narrative arc as a curving line (the reason it is called an arc), you can see that the reader begins in one place, then follows the narrative structure upward to

"In simplest terms, narrative structure consists of a beginning, a middle, and an end.

a "climax," then gently downward to the ending, where you leave them somewhere they have never been before.

In reality, a narrative arc tends to have many ups and downs in the middle, and many smaller arcs within the larger arc. But overall, it should lead the reader up an emotional hill to a climax, then gently back down again, leaving them somewhere new.

What Do Narrative Structure and Arc Look Like in Fiction?

Though it is also important in non-fiction, narrative structure and arc are generally easiest to spot in fiction, so let's start there.

In a novel, a narrative structure usually includes setting the scene and introducing a complication (the beginning), all the things that happen as a result of the complication and the characters' actions (the middle), and a climax and resolution (the end).

For example, in *The Lord of The Rings*, the beginning introduces us to a humble hobbit who is having a birthday party (setting the scene), after which his mentor gifts him a magical ring. A wizard shows up and tells him the ring is much more powerful than he thought and must be destroyed (the complication). That's the beginning.

Then a lot of things happen: The hobbit agrees to go on the ring-destroying mission, a bunch of dwarfs show up to help, they get attacked and stalked by all sorts of evil things, elves and humans join their mission, wars unfold, and so on. As the story progresses, things get harder and harder, the stakes get higher, and the main task (destroy the ring) becomes increasingly complicated to the point of being almost impossible. Then there is a huge central conflict that leads to the climax at the top of the narrative arc. That's the middle.

Finally, at the height of the climax, the hobbit and one loyal hobbit friend succeed in disposing of the ring, the war is won, and everyone goes home changed by the events of the middle. That's the end.

The narrative structure of Lord of The Rings creates a narrative arc that takes the reader on an emotional journey with the characters. From curiosity and enjoyment at the beginning, the reader moves through fear, anxiety, exhilaration, pride, conflict, solidarity, and many other emotions with many smaller narrative arcs within the main arc.

Near the end, readers experience significant emotional tension as they watch the characters contend with seemingly impossible odds. Then they feel the release of that tension as the characters overcome those odds through strength, determination, and a few twists of the plot. And now one descends the downward curve of the arc toward the very end where to discover that the characters are very different people than they were at the beginning, and the reader's feelings about them are likewise different.

You may even feel differently in your own life, from having navigated these fictional experiences with characters you loved, hated, identified with, detested, feared, longed for, or wanted to be friends with.

You, and the characters, are in a different place than where you began, and the narrative arc, built through the means of the narrative structure, got you there.

What Do Narrative Structure and Arc Look Like In Non-Fiction?

Non-fiction relies on narrative structure just as much as fiction does. It includes how you introduce your material (the beginning), how you communicate your main points (the middle), and how you wrap it all up (the end).

Narrative structure is how you guide your readers through the processes and information you want them to understand. You'll use narrative structure to guide them through the complexity of the middle portions of your book. You're navigating narrative structure when you ask yourself questions like, should I talk about narrative arc before I show you how to organize an outline? Do readers need to know how to set up your document before you begin writing your manuscript?

A clear, clean, orderly narrative structure is often (though not always) ideal for nonfiction informational books. However, that doesn't mean that narrative arc can't or shouldn't also play a role. Just because it's orderly doesn't mean it can't provide an emotional journey. In fact, without an emotional journey, it will read like a dry manual, and very few readers will actually want to consume it.

In fiction, narrative arc defines the forward momentum of the story. In informational nonfiction, it defines the reader's emotional journey as they consume the material you present. It is almost always there, but it is often more subtle than in fiction.

Your arc may begin by generating curiosity or hope for a solution, and then lead readers into the middle where they embark on a journey of understanding their problem more deeply, which may increase their pain as they realize the depths of the problem. You may raise questions they don't have answers to, leave them hanging (strategically) and only later fulfill promises you made early on while opening up new questions to keep them interested. At the end, they should feel that the tension you created along the way has been relieved and has left them somewhere new and better than where they started.

The ancient Greeks called this "catharsis." It's the emotional release you feel after the climax gives way to the resolution, and you can have it in nonfiction just as much as in fiction.

Many non-fiction books do fail the narrative arc test, though. A boring, unfulfilling, or badly constructed arc will send readers away as soon as they feel they understand the basic principles of the book.

But some non-fiction books step up quite nicely.

For instance, in *Good to Great*, we are presented with the idea that some companies outperform other companies by a great deal (setting the scene), and they all have one thing in common (the "complication" or, in this case, the hook). That's the beginning. Then the book explores in detail what that one thing is and presents a method for achieving it for your own company. That's the middle. Finally, it tells you where you can learn more and what results you can expect to see from your efforts. That's the end. Put together, that is the overall narrative structure of *Good to Great,* and the narrative structure creates a narrative arc.

The arc of *Good to Great* takes you from curiosity to understanding why your company is only "good," to greater and greater complexity of that understanding, to pain or apprehension as you question your existing approach to business, to understanding your strengths and weaknesses more deeply through a new lens, to a desire to apply the book's principles, and leaves you at the end feeling that maybe your company can be so much more than it is, if you can re-envision it according to the book's lessons.

A great nonfiction narrative arc can generate curiosity and/or tension at the beginning, interest and emotion throughout, and a sense of catharsis and resolution at the end. The reader may feel satisfied, inspired, or that something important can be different because of your book. They may feel motivated to take action on what you have suggested.

The Elements of Great Narrative Structure in Nonfiction

Remember that narrative structure is deceptively simple: A beginning, a middle, and an end.

The magic lies in what happens within each stage.

In this next section, I've done my best to condense the most important aspects of each element of nonfiction narrative structure into simple terms. View these as building blocks for creating a narrative arc that pulls your readers through the book and changes them along the way.

That said, it's important to remember that every book is different. Approach this section as guidelines, not immutable rules.

The Beginning

The beginning of your book is arguably the most important part. Readers often make a decision to read a book by looking at the first few pages. If you lose them here, you lose them. If you grab them here, they are much more likely to stick with you throughout.

Here is some of the heavy lifting the beginning portion of your book must do:

- Draw the reader in quickly and hold their interest.
- Connect with the reader where they are (not where you want them to be).
- Set up the "promise" of the book.
- Introduce the reader to your authentic, compelling, entirely unique voice.
- Create curiosity by leading them in but not giving everything away all at once.
- Raise questions within the reader that make them want more.
- Convince them that you are a trustworthy companion capable of fulfilling the promises you've made and answering the questions you've raised.

That is a lot for one small section of a book to do. And yet, it must do it, and it must do it in an entirely fresh, new, authentic-to-you way. That is a tall order.

To help you along, I've provided some tips below for creating a compelling opening. However, these especially should be viewed as potential options, not hard and fast rules. Every beginning must be entirely unique, or it will fail the first test. Review these, and later, when you are ready to write your beginning, you can apply those that work for you.

- Understand where your reader is coming from, and connect immediately with what you know is important to them.
- Consider starting with a story, a motivating insight, or an interesting fact. This should be directly connected to the main point of your book, without giving too much away.
- If you start with a story, leave them hanging a little at the end. Don't give them the full satisfaction of completion. Save the satisfaction for the end of your book. This draws out their curiosity and gives them one more reason to keep reading.
- If you start with an insight, statistic, or fact, don't give them immediate resolution. Choose an insight that leaves them with as many questions as answers and makes them want to learn more.
- The pattern here is: Connect with them, inspire or motivate them, then leave something unresolved. Don't give all the answers away in the first few pages. No spoilers!
- Consider addressing your readers directly. People like to feel seen and heard. You may want to immediately

address the reasons they came to your book and assure them that you understand their problems and their position. Make them feel less alone.

- Lean hard into your own unique voice. Who you are is why your readers are here. Be all of you. And, by the way, it's okay to be freaking weird!

The Art of Impossible starts with the premise that some people achieve seemingly impossible things, and they all share some commonalities that we can emulate. This immediately draws the reader in and makes them curious: What are those commonalities, and can I be like that?

This book started by connecting with the very human desire to be heard, and the fears many potential authors have on that score. It left the reader, I hope, with the confidence that they can be heard, and the inspiration to find out how in the rest of the book.

One last thing to know about the beginning is that even though it's the beginning, you usually shouldn't begin by writing the beginning. Introductions and conclusions are the hardest parts of the book to write, and they can feel intimidating. Furthermore, you may not know what the most impactful way to start the book is until you've written out a good deal of the middle.

Very often, the easiest and best way to write a book is to begin in the middle and come back to the beginning at the end (and then write the end after that).

As I will throughout this book, I encourage you to lean into writing in whatever order feels good and right to you. So write the intro first if that feels good to you, but don't stress if you don't know how to write it till much later.

The Middle

The middle is where most of the action or "meat" of your book occurs. The complexity introduced at the beginning unfolds and expands. In fiction, this is where characters act and respond, while the environment and situation evolve around them. It's where they interact with other characters and new things happen that complicate earlier things. It can be messy and complex, but it will (usually) have a forward momentum that drives the plot.

In nonfiction, the middle is where you unfold the answers to questions you raised at the beginning, further explore the insights or statistics you introduce, and fulfill the promises you made at the beginning. Your narrative structure may include step by step instructions, examples, explanations, and further information and statistics. It may include stories to illustrate and refine your points.

A solid narrative structure for the middle of a nonfiction informational book may contain:

- Three to seven main points, in a logical, easy to follow order. These main points may each form a chapter or "part" (Part I, Part II, etc, as in this book). Each larger part may contain smaller parts, such as Part I, Chapter Three, where we currently are in this book.

- The top level main points may be steps in a process (as in this book), high level concepts (consider *Traction* by Gino Wickman), or a mix of both (*Good to Great* is an example of this).

- If your book reflects a service you offer, your middle section may lay out your offering in a self-serve order that mirrors the process you deliver your clients (this book is an example).

- Within each main section, your arc will contain smaller points that support the main point, as well as stories and other information to help the reader and hold their interest. These may be broken down into chapters, subsections, sub-subsections, sidebars, graphs, charts, and other elements within each larger section.

- Your middle may contain many types of information in many different formats, including questions and answers, case studies, exercises, step by step guides, examples, and inspirational or motivational content.

- The order of your narrative may be chronological, following a step by step progression of "how to do it."

- Or it may spiral outward from key points and then back again to the center.
- Or it may continue to draw the story, facts, or metaphor from the beginning through the main points as in narrative nonfiction.

While the beginning and the end are the hardest parts to write, the middle is the most time-consuming. It can also be challenging to maintain a narrative arc that holds the reader's attention through the potentially long slog of everything you have to share.

This can be achieved by ensuring that your main arc contains many smaller arcs as well: Chapters with beginnings that raise curiosity, middles that pull the reader along, and endings that provide catharsis and resolution, while driving the reader forward to the next section. Vignettes with compelling beginnings, middles, and ends. How-tos with valuable beginnings, middles, and ends. And so on.

Take a moment to flip to the table of contents for this book. You will very quickly see the narrative structure of this book, as well as its series of arcs within arcs. You'll see that there is an introduction, three sections in the middle, and a conclusion. You'll see that each middle section (Part I, Part II, Part III) addresses one major portion of the writing process. Then you'll see that within each Part, there are chapters that form the narrative structure of that part. Within each chapter, there are subsections that form the narrative structure of the chapter. Within each subsection there may be bullet lists, case studies, and short stories, each with their own arc.

It's a lot of arcs. But don't let this intimidate you. Start with your high-level, big picture arc. You will refine the main arc as you go, and develop the smaller arcs within at each iteration of the process.

In the next chapter, we will begin developing your working outline. The working outline will show you the larger framework of your narrative structure, without forcing you to get bogged down too early in the details of smaller arcs.

The Ending

Though often the shortest part of the book, the ending does almost as much heavy lifting as the beginning. A great ending leaves the reader feeling satisfied that the promise of the book has been fulfilled. It may give them an "aha!" moment that evokes substantial emotion, such as relief, inspiration, joy, motivation, or simple delight with a memorable take-away.

Our brains are curious animals, with funny little patterns that are consistent across our species. One of those patterns is that we tend to remember beginnings and endings, but not so much middles. Yet, the middles are critical for us to enjoy the beginnings and the endings, and the ending is often critical for us to enjoy the middle.

If you read fiction, you may have had this experience: You're enjoying a book very much. It has a promising beginning, and a riveting middle. Then you get to the end, and the ending is poorly conceived, leaves too many loose ends, and feels deeply unsatisfying. Now you look back at the beginning and the middle, and no longer feel that you have enjoyed the book.

No matter how much you enjoyed the rest of the ride, the ending ruined it all. It's like taking a gorgeous drive through the countryside only to arrive at your destination in a Walmart parking lot in a desolate deserted suburb with a cheap roach-infested half-abandoned motel to sleep in.

A popular example of this phenomenon is the last season of *Game of Thrones*. With more than 700 hours of stunning cinematography, riveting storylines, and unforgettable characters, the epic television series captivated the imaginations of millions of people. There were so many arcs within arcs within the main arc of the series that it would be nearly impossible to count them all.

But the last season was rushed, poorly conceived, and failed to deliver on the promises of the series. Viewers felt cheated because beloved characters acted out of character and made decisions that made no sense, the plot rushed forward precipitously with no clear connection to the events of the earlier seasons, and many of the arcs that were developed throughout the series were left hanging, without a satisfactory conclusion.

While the series is still beloved and well-watched, years later, it remains deeply marred by its bad ending.

So you can see that if you mess up the ending of your book, you can mess up the whole book. It's that important.

Don't let this scare you, though. Let it motivate you to take your time here, to pay attention to it, and to get it right.

Just like the beginning, you don't have to know what your ending will say or what it will be until the very end of your process. I always encourage clients to wait to write the ending, to not even include it in their first draft. Leave it blank till you've written the rest and revised it a few times, until you feel deeply confident that you know what you want to leave your readers with.

I drink my own medicine. As of version 5.3 of this manuscript, the conclusion section is blank. As of version 7.0, it is written but needs editing. I hope before I'm done that I'll manage to bring it home. You be the judge.

When you do get ready to write your conclusion, here are some tips that can help you make it as strong as it can be.

- The ending is in the beginning: Always look back to the beginning to ensure you've wrapped up all the loose ends and fulfilled all your promises. You may also find clues here for how to bring the book to a fulfilling end.

- Create balance between the beginning and the ending by mirroring, reflecting, amplifying, or completing the themes introduced in the beginning.

- If you told a story at the beginning and left the reader hanging, consider using the conclusion to tell the end of the story in a way that wraps up all the points you made in the middle. If it feels right, you can rewrite the beginning to allow this to happen.

- You can do the same thing with statistics, information, and other types of openings. Leave a little bit of it hanging at the beginning, then bring the reader back to the beginning at the end to wrap it up.

- The ending should provide some new insight that is supported by the material in the middle, such that the reader sees the clear connection between everything they have read and the conclusion you have drawn.

- The ending should be amplified by everything in the middle.

- The ending should not go off on new tangents or introduce new material, but rather draw from everything before to provide a final set of insights and conclusions.

- Wrap up loose ends! Don't leave the reader hanging on any key points.
- You may want to conclude with a take-away section that summarizes the key points and reminds the reader where to look for the supporting material.
- You may want to end with an inspiration, an exhortation, or motivation to your readers.
- If you have directly addressed readers at the beginning and/or throughout, it is a good idea to return to that direct address here and offer them your heartfelt well wishes as they seek to implement what they've learned.

An example of a book that does a good job with the conclusion is the massive hit, *Untamed,* by Glennon Doyle. In the prologue she tells a story of seeing a cheetah in captivity and feeling a kinship with its raw power contained in an environment that is wrong for it. The middle is filled with complications in her personal and professional life, stories of staying in relationships, jobs, and other socially constructed cages too long, and how she finally found her way free of them. In the final paragraph of the book, she proclaims that she will never again stay in a relationship or situation that requires her to abandon herself.

It finishes with the memorable last line: "Because I have just remembered that the sun is shining, the breeze is cool, and these doors, they're not even locked."

Note the simplicity of this line, and how its impact depends on the set-up of the beginning and the complications of the middle, yet leaves the reader breathless and stunned, yet ready to walk out of their own unlocked cages and into the sun and the breeze.

Now you can see why the conclusion is both critically important, and dependent on the beginning and the middle, and why you probably want to wait to the end of your process to write it.

Narrative Tension

Oops. I told you there were only three elements to a narrative arc, but now I'm telling you there's one more: Narrative tension. Never fear, it's not an extra step, it's a result to look out for. Narrative tension is what happens when your narrative arc is successful.

Narrative tension keeps your reader engaged. When you just have to turn the page, just have to watch the next episode, just have to see what will happen next–that's narrative tension.

There are a variety of ways to create narrative tension. Even the driest of dry technical manuals can contain narrative tension that makes their audience want to read the next chapter to learn what that chapter will hold.

Narrative tension is a type of curiosity. It's a promise of something to come, without revealing the full nature of the thing.

It's the cliffhanger at the end of a show's season. It's the promise to solve a problem at the end of a promotional webinar. It's the satisfaction at the end of a chapter that you've learned what you wanted to learn, combined with the title of the next chapter that promises you'll learn another thing you want to know when you turn that page.

Narrative tension can include dropping "hints" (foreshadowing) in a work of fiction or memoir, without revealing the answer till later. It's when a character starts writing a letter to their best friend, and you don't yet know if they're going to tell them about their spouse cheating. Or you can see that they are going to tell them, but you don't know what the consequences of that will be.

In non-fiction, narrative tension can be created by introducing concepts with the promise that you'll talk more about them later. Narrative tension can even be created in a table of contents, when the chapter headings make the reader want to know more (see: the TOC for this book).

Narrative tension is not only a great thing to include: It's essential.

When narrative tension fails, so does the book. Most readers will not continue past a few pages or even sentences if you have not inspired curiosity, interest, fear, or some other strong emotion via narrative tension.

In most cases, each bit of narrative tension must eventually be resolved. This builds trust with the reader and helps them feel satisfied that they've gotten what they came for.

Overlapping your narrative tension so that you relieve one bit only after introducing a new bit can keep your reader going all the way to the end. Just make sure you resolve all of it by the conclusion.

An outstanding developmental editor can help you see where your work needs more tension, and help you develop it effectively.

EXERCISE: WATCH FOR NARRATIVE ARCS

Estimated Time: However much you want!

Your homework for this section is to start paying attention to narrative structure and arc in the media you consume. Whether it's books, movies, social media content, or otherwise, see if you can identify the beginning, the middle, and the end of things.

When you are engaged and enthralled by something, see if you can understand the emotional journey that is keeping you hooked. If you get bored or don't finish reading something, see if you can identify what was lacking in the emotional journey.

You can continue this exercise throughout your writing journey and the rest of your life. Paying attention to how other storytellers succeed (and don't succeed) at narrative structure and arc will teach you a great deal about how you want to build your structure and arcs.

CHAPTER FOUR:

YOUR OUTLINE
charts the route

Now that you understand narrative structure more clearly, you are ready to craft a working outline. Your outline will reveal the broad strokes of your main narrative structure, plus a high-level view of some of the smaller arcs within each section.

A solid working outline charts the course for the duration of your writing journey. It will help prevent you from taking unnecessary detours, getting stuck in common traps, or getting lost along the way. It also provides the freedom to work on whichever part of the journey you want at any time, knowing that it all takes you to the destination in the end.

Planning versus "pantsing"

In the writing community, there is a decades-old raging debate over whether it is better to plan your book first, or simply "pants" it–i.e., write by the seat of your pants.

This is especially controversial in fiction, where even famous authors seem to range in approach from "I don't know, I just have an idea and start writing" to "I map out every detail of the plot and then fill it in."

When writing fiction, I personally tend to pants pretty heavily, letting the characters and situation carry the story wherever it wants to go.

In non-fiction, an outline is critical in order for a cohesive book to emerge. A working outline keeps you on task and focused, and makes it possible to create an effective writing plan, which is another key to actually completing the manuscript.

Why You Need a Working Outline

A working outline can make the difference between years of struggle, and effectively completing your book within months or even weeks.

Bill (name changed to protect privacy) came to me with a draft he'd been working on for years. It was a mess, and he knew it. He just couldn't get it to do what he wanted it to do, not even with the help of several professionals he had hired and fired. But, he mustered a little more courage and brought himself to the workshop.

Magic happened.

Everything he needed was already in the draft. He just hadn't figured out how to organize it yet, because he didn't understand the key elements of narrative structure. I asked questions, and listened to his answers.

Collaborating with him, I drew out the structure that worked for this particular book and his particular audience. Within weeks, Bill's draft was pared down and rewritten into a manuscript that fulfilled his original vision and delivered on the promise he'd made to himself and his readers.

It is sadly common for authors to work on drafts for years and sometimes decades and never finish. It's frustrating, and I hate to see it. Your book deserves to be completed.

In the same way that a route map is important for reaching a physical destination, your working outline is an important key to completing your book writing journey. At the end of this chapter, you'll find a process that will help you produce an effective working outline. But first, I want you to understand how you'll use it during your writing process.

How To Use A Working Outline

The word "working" in "working outline" is operative here. The outline is for working with. It is not a straitjacket. It will shift and change as you go, so keep that in mind while you're creating it: It doesn't have to be perfect. It just needs to be functional.

Here's how you'll use it:

- It will provide you with a framework of concepts and ideas you plan to cover in the book.
- This forms a series of "chunks" of writing you have to do.
- You can write these chunks *in any order that appeals to you*!

This latter point is really important. One of the ways that a lot of writers get stuck, is thinking they have to follow a linear path in their writing process. They get to a part that feels boring or uninspiring, and find they just can't make themselves do it anymore.

Turn that on its head! Lean into the pleasure and the fun. Your brain needs dopamine to keep itself motivated. If you start to feel unmotivated, change gears and do something easy and inspiring. Your working outline provides the perfect tool for this. Take a look at it, see what part calls out to you, and work on that instead. Trust the outline to remind you where you are and what else you need to do, and free your creative brain to focus on what it wants to do.

When you approach the work this way, it will feel lighter and easier. The sections that feel hard at one time, will feel easier later when you've done the easy parts. And the parts that still feel hard toward the end, will feel less hard because you're so close to the finish line.

Now that you understand how you'll use the working outline, let's get started putting it together, shall we?

EXERCISE: CREATE YOUR WORKING OUTLINE

Estimated Time: 90-120 minutes

For this exercise, carve out between 90 minutes and two hours when you can work undisturbed. This exercise uses both the creative and the critical sides of your brain, so make sure you've chosen a time when you can be in a relaxed state with a clear and focused mind. Use a note-taking tool of your choice, but make sure you can see and edit your notes in real time. Make sure your North Star Statement is visible in your work area.

Step One: Brain Dump

Spend a few minutes reviewing your North Star Statement. If you notice edits you'd like to make to the statement, do so at this time. It should feel really good to you before you begin.

Then, take a deep breath, and review the questions below. Answer them in any order that feels right to you. Answer with as much detail, or as little, as you like. Allow whatever comes to mind to flow out. Don't censor yourself, and don't worry if you repeat yourself. Repetition is not a bad thing–it helps us see where our key ideas live and what's important to focus on.

Working Outline Questions

- What do *you* want your reader to know?
- What do your *readers* want to know?
- What questions do people like your readers always ask?
- Where do they get stuck?
- How do you help them get unstuck?
- What are the main points you want to make?
- What stories can you think of that support your main points?
- Do you have evidence or data that backs up your claims?
- What images, graphs, or visuals could bring your ideas to life?

Spend at least twenty minutes on this step, up to an hour. There are no wrong answers, and it's okay if you don't have answers to all the questions. Focus on those that you do.

If you find you are done in less than twenty minutes, go back and focus on each question again, to generate more thoughts and ideas. There's always a little deeper you can go.

However, don't overthink this. If you find yourself drawing out the process, check in with yourself at around 45 minutes. Look at the list of questions and focus on any remaining ones that feel important to you, then call it quits at an hour. Knowing when to quit is an important ingredient in getting the work actually complete.

Step Two: Organize

I love the "wow" moment authors get when they see that what they thought was just "rambling" can turn into a co-hesive structure with a narrative arc and meaningful sub-stance. That's where you're headed next.

Your answers to the previous questions will provide you with all the raw material you need to fashion a solid working outline. Set aside about 30 to 45 minutes for this step, but don't fret if it takes you up to 90 minutes.

Review your North Star Statement again. Review your notes from the previous step. Your task now is to start moving sections of your notes around to lump similar ideas together. You can use the copy & paste function in a word processor, a pen and ink, or literal scissors and tape to do this.

You will be using a more critical part of your brain for this process, but don't overthink it. If it feels like it belongs together, lump it together. Here are some types of lumps you might choose:

- Chronological lumps: Stories, ideas, and concepts can be organized from earliest to latest

- Linear process lumps: Similar to a chronological order, a process lump is a start to finish lump, organized along the lines of "step one," "step two," etc.
- Similar idea lumps: Related concepts can go together regardless of chronology
- Problems and their solutions: You can lump ideas that are related to the same problems and solutions together

Allow the material itself to "tell" you what wants to go where, and rearrange as much as you need to until it starts to feel right. You are aiming for between 3 and 7 main categories of information. If you have more categories than that, you either have material for another book, or you haven't finished grouping the material yet. Keep going.

Once you have your main categories, look again at the material within each one. Can you now categorize the material in each section into smaller "lumps"? Keep doing this until you feel like you've got an overall structure that makes sense for you.

Step Three: Summarize

Now, go back to the chunks of information you've organized. For each main point, write a brief summary, and turn it into a bullet point. For the smaller lumps of information, make them bullet points under the main points.

Your summaries can be one or two words, or they can be a short sentence. Do not write more than a brief sentence for each one. If you need more than a sentence, you either have more than one idea, or you haven't clarified the central idea yet.

You may find that you have a great deal of good material left over after you've summarized. Don't delete this juicy stuff! Move it down into its own section. You'll park it in your parking lot later (see chapter 8), but for now just set it aside.

Keep writing your summaries and bulleting them until you have all of your main ideas organized into an at-a-glance format that makes sense to you.

Magic: You now have a working outline.

Take a good look at it as a whole. Does it hang together? Does it fulfill the promise of your North Star Statement? Is this a route map that will take you and your readers where you want to go?

Massage the outline until you can say "yes" to all of the above.

Some working outlines consist of a simple set of brief bullet points. Some working outlines are quite elaborate indeed, with detailed points and sub points under the main headings. Anywhere within this spectrum is fine, as long as it feels clear and makes sense to you. Just don't get bogged down trying to make it perfect. It will never be perfect. The important thing is to create a framework that *you* can work with.

Step Four: Print It Out

Remember, the brain likes to focus on things that are right in front of it. What you place in front of it is what it will fixate on.

When your outline looks the way you want it, print it out, and post it where you can see it, near your North Star Statement. Then take a nice deep breath and pat yourself on the back. Whew. You have come a long way already, and you're almost to the starting line!

REST STOP

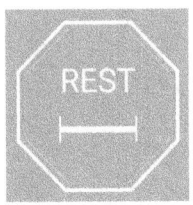

Chapter Five

YOUR WRITING PLAN
provides your personal operating instructions

Your writing plan is one of the key tools that differentiates completed manuscripts from projects that go on for decades. It's a little like the operating manual for your vehicle, except you are the vehicle on this journey.

Your writing plan should work with how you work, account for your lifestyle, and map out how you will operate yourself in order to get the work of your manuscript complete.

I wrote my first novel while my children were very young. I set an alarm every morning for 5am, because it was the only time of day I was confident I would not be interrupted. I would write for an hour, then begin the morning chores. I did this for months, every day, no matter whether I was sick, on vacation, or overwhelmed with everything else in life. At their bedtime, I'd read a chapter or two of the emerging draft to my children. Then I'd crash and start all over the next day.

This process doesn't work for me today. As my body has matured over the years, I find that waking at 5am isn't conducive to my energy flows. And, importantly, it's no longer necessary for me to be awake before everyone else in order to be productive. My teenagers respect "do not enter" signs, so my flow can be attuned to my own schedule rather than theirs.

Every person at every stage of life has a unique way that their energies and circumstances work. Jamie Sams speaks of the "hour of power" in *Sacred Path Cards*, a book of teachings from her indigenous ancestors. There's a time of day in which each person's energy flow is strongest, and it can change for you over the course of your life.

Let go of the idea that you have to be an early bird to get this work done just because that's what some self-appointed "guru" said, or that you need to have lots of big open spaces in your life before you can begin.

I've worked with authors from all walks of life, from CEOs of major hospital systems, to spiritual leaders, single moms, entrepreneurs, burlesque dancers, and bankers. Every one of them has a different flow of energy and time in their life. Most of them have completed an initial draft in an average of five to ten hours a week over five weeks, and a complete manuscript in 90 to 180 days. Each of them followed a different pattern of work.

One of them worked on their first draft for ninety minutes each weekday morning, with weekends off. Another preferred to work in the afternoons, and committed to an average of five hours a week, and chose which days based on how they felt each day. Another found the weeks too busy for creative work, and instead committed to six hours each weekend. Yet another took one week off from work, flew to Mexico, ate papayas and limes, and simply worked like mad till the first draft was done. We should all be so lucky!

Your writing plan will help you flow within the unique constraints and opportunities of your life. It's a tool for holding yourself accountable to getting your draft done in a way that works with your life instead of against it.

The writing plan also enables you to measure your progress, so you can see that you are meeting your targets, and get those critical dopamine hits each time you do.

EXERCISE: CREATE YOUR WRITING PLAN

Estimated Time: 60 minutes

Step One: Understand The Ninety-Day Framework

Writing a book is a big project. Some people take a year, or ten years, or even thirty years. *Lord of the Rings* took Tolkien twelve years to write, and five years to publish. (Stop beating yourself up for not having finished your masterwork yet!)

But most of us aren't trying to completely reinvent a country's mythology, create fifteen fully fleshed fictional languages and a companion volume of fake cultural history for an entire continent, while also teaching college courses and drinking ale with C.S. Lewis. Though the latter is undoubtedly worth striving for.

And, even if we are, it doesn't have to take seventeen years. Tolkien himself was frustrated with the slow progress of his work. Maybe if he'd had a solid writing plan and expert support, he could have produced more work. What I wouldn't give to go back in time and be his book midwife!

Regardless of how we might rewrite history if we could, *you* deserve support and structure that means your book *won't* take twelve years. In fact, you can probably achieve a complete manuscript that you're proud of in 90 days. Even with your crazy life.

How do I know? Because most of my program clients do.

For most people, 90 days is absolutely achievable *and desirable*, and authors who work with me consistently (often to their own amazement) prove it. CEOs, business owners, single moms, mental health professionals, bankers, accountants: Ninety days.

Why 90 days?

Ninety days is the length of time that the human brain can easily stay focused on a single goal or theme. Gino Wickman's excellent book *Traction* discusses the science behind this and lays out the 90-day structure that I use to plan most of my business and some of my life.

Science says: After ninety days, the mind starts to wander and attention fades, along with motivation.

A ninety-day target helps you stay focused, and provides you with an "end date" you can look forward to. If you're pushing yourself to complete a big project (like a manuscript!) the ninety-day timeframe lets your body and brain know that there's a point at which it will be allowed to rest again.

Remember that life happens and 90 days can turn into longer stretches. Some authors just need more time to incubate, and that's okay. Ninety days is a great starting target, not a straitjacket. If you don't make it? No worries: Take a rest, then set another 90-day target.

Within the first ninety days, there are shorter periods or "sprints." The biggest sprint is the first draft period, which in my program is generally about five weeks. The hardest sprint is the first revision period, which is generally about two weeks. The most fun sprint for most people is the last leg of the journey, when you can almost touch the smell of victory.

Now, let's take a look at how we're going to break down the 90 days into sprints.

Step Two: Understand The Writing Stages

There are three key stages to producing a solid manuscript, and each stage requires a different part of your brain and a different approach to the work. These stages are:

1. Produce a rough draft (write like mad!)
2. Revise (structural improvement)
3. Edit (clean it up)

We'll talk about these stages more in parts II (rough draft) and III (revising and editing), but for now what you need to understand is how to make room for each stage in your writing plan. A solid 90-day plan that works for many of the authors in my program starts with this basic rhythm:

- Weeks 1-5: Write your first draft
- Weeks 6-7: *Rest* while a professional prepares Developmental Feedback
- Weeks 8-9: Revise
- Weeks 10-11: *Rest* while a professional provides Editorial Feedback
- Weeks 12-13: Edit

You can adjust this rhythm to accommodate circumstances and your unique needs. For instance, you may want to extend the timeline by a week or two to account for vacations, holidays, or other planned activities that might interfere with your ability to focus. Or, you can plan those things during your rest periods.

The important thing is to build a rhythm that works for and with you, and to remember that if your process extends past 90 days, you'll need to step back at that point and recalibrate a new 90-day plan.

A 90-Day Writing Plan Rhythm

- 5 weeks to a first draft: Furiously get words down on paper.
- 2 weeks to let your brain rest. Hand the draft to a professional developmental editor for feedback.

- 2 weeks to revise the structure, organization, and storytelling, and to bring your voice out more clearly. For most authors, this is the hardest part of the process but also the most gratifying.
- 2 weeks of rest. Have an editor provide additional feedback during this time.
- 2 weeks for another round of edits to clean up the manuscript.

Step Three: Set Your First Draft Targets

In order to harness your brain's power of focus, provide it with specific, achievable daily and weekly goals during the first draft stage. This will generate hits of dopamine, the brain's reward chemical that also drives focus and motivation.

Having targets will also help you identify when you are behind schedule, so you can make adjustments to either your work plan or your timeline.

It's common to use either word-based daily targets or time-based goals, but I have found it most productive to use a hybrid that focuses on three key performance indicators (KPIs):

- Time spent
- Word count (number of words written)
- Outline sections completed

Time spent is a good DAILY measure, because it removes the pressure to accomplish something specific that day. Daily word counts can be counterproductive because some days you will write like mad and the words will flow like water from a fresh mountain spring, and some days you will sit staring into space for half an hour before you can write down a single word.

Time-based daily goals allow you to manage your time effectively and still feel productive on days when your writing process involves work that isn't strictly producing words. Thinking, research, re-reading, musing, and allowing the creative juices to flow in their own good time are all valid and important parts of the process, and a daily time-based goal makes room for that.

However, time-based goals alone have two key weaknesses: They can encourage unproductive "wandering," and they don't provide you with a clear picture of when you will be "done." So to address that, I advise a WEEKLY word-count based target. This enables you to check each week whether you're making the progress you want to make, and adjust accordingly.

Finally, I advise a BIWEEKLY check in against your outline, to ensure you're filling it in at a pace that will enable you to complete your manuscript on time. In the end, your word count is not what matters. Whether you've said what you needed to say is. So outline check-ins help ensure you're getting through the material at a pace that makes sense for you.

Now, we'll take a look at how to set these targets effectively. There are a lot of steps and a good bit of math in this section, but bear with it. It will pay off big time.

1. Set a Target Word Count for Your Manuscript

In order to set weekly word count goals, you need a rough estimate of how long your finished manuscript will be.

This is a much harder question than it sounds like on the surface, and it's not the same for everyone. If you run an internet search on the question, you may come up with a number that *seems* to be the consensus for nonfiction books, of roughly 50,000 to 70,000 words.

"Seems" is the operative word here.

Ah, internet. Someday we will look back fondly on the days when search engines served up the same regurgitated, plagiarized, AI-generated white bread "content" over and over for page after page after page. But today is not that day.

Now I'm going to tell you the truth, and you are going to check my facts against your own bookshelves.

A *huge* number of popular and critically acclaimed nonfiction books fall *well* outside this "recommended" range. Some are much, much longer. My favorite nonfiction book of the 21st century is Robin Wall Kimmerer's wildly successful *Braiding Sweetgrass*, which clocks in at a whopping (roughly) 122,000+ words. Holy moly.

Her first book, *Gathering Moss*, was a modest (by comparison) 42,000 (which is under the length generally recommended by search engine "gurus"–go figure).

Simon Sinek's beautiful little volume, *Together is Better*, contains fewer than 3,000 words.

All of these highly successful books were published by the same traditional publishers who insist that your nonfiction manuscripts must be between 50,000 and 70,000 words.

The odds are high that if you go look at your bookshelves right now, you will readily find nonfiction works that fall well outside the "recommended" word count on either side.

The truth is, there is no "right" word count for a nonfiction manuscript.

The 50,000-70,000 word "rule" is utter bollocks.

Sort of.

It *is* true that most traditional publishers, for first-time authors, are looking for manuscripts that fall inside this range. That is not because it is the best possible range for a nonfiction manuscript. It is because it is easier for them to print, market, and sell books from a first-time author in that range. This will NOT necessarily be true for you.

Commercial publishers are looking to make the most money on the least amount of work (for them). They are less concerned about changing the world (or their author's lives) and more concerned about what mediocre pablum is selling today.

Your book is not going to be mediocre pablum, is it? So stop worrying about whether it's the "right" length to join the ranks of mediocre pablum.

Instead, focus on making it as long as it needs to be to give your readers the gifts you have promised to give them.

No longer, no shorter.

However, for your writing plan you still want to have a general idea of how long the book is likely to be. In most cases, for my clients, a manuscript between 15,000 and 65,000 words is about right. This is long enough to feel substantial and have that "I wrote a BOOK" heft to it when you hold it in your hands, long enough to say everything you want your readers to know, and short enough to hold their attention.

At the end of each Roadmap Workshop, I take a moment to provide my professional opinion of how many words the author's specific finished book is likely to be. I'm usually right within 5,000 words or so. If you're working with me, I'll do the same for you.

Otherwise, try this. Pick a number. Why not 20,000? Twenty thousand is a lovely, round number to head toward.

Let's go with that for the purposes of this exercise. Then, take a look at your outline and feel into whether it looks and feels like a long book or a short book. If you expect it to be a tight, sharp little volume with just a few key home runs, adjust your number down. If your subject requires more space to expand into in order to fulfill your reader's needs and your vision, adjust your number up.

It's okay if you're wrong. We're just estimating for planning purposes.

Write your number down on a sheet of paper and label it "Manuscript Target Word Count." For the purposes of the examples in this exercise, I'll use a target word count of 20,000.

2. Estimate How Much Time Your First Draft Will Take to Write

To set your initial daily or weekly time-based targets, you need to know roughly how long it will take you to write that first draft. Your typing speed will have an impact on this, but it isn't the most critical factor.

I can type 120 words a minute when I really get going, and this does mean that I write faster…when I really get going.

But a lot of "writing" is actually thinking while staring.

Or rereading to remind yourself what you've already covered.

Or looking up that data point to be sure you know what you're talking about.

If you've done a lot of writing in the past, you may already have some sense of how long it will take you to produce 20,000 words. Otherwise, you're going to have to do some guessing, and then adjust as you go.

Most of our clients find that they can complete their initial draft in roughly one to two hours per weekday, over about five weeks. As of this exact moment in time writing my initial draft of this book, I have vomited up 7,239 words onto the page in not quite four hours. At this current pace, I'll have a complete first draft (of 20,000 words, my target) (Note: the final draft ended up slightly more than 40,000… oops) in approximately eleven hours. Like I said, I'm speedy. I'm both a fast typist, and a professional writer who has been doing this for more than thirty years (but who still doesn't know how many words a final draft will be).

A new author who recently completed her full manuscript (as of this writing) wrote her 40,000-word first draft in about three weeks over a long vacation, by writing for about three hours a day. She is not a professional writer, nor a speed typist (she admitted that she still hunts and pecks). She spent about 45 hours total to reach a first draft.

In short, it can be hard to know how long you need until you get into a rhythm. But there are some consistent ranges that work for most authors. Pick a number between 25 and 45, based on your speed and your target length, and you'll likely get into the ballpark.

Write this number down below the Target Word Count and label it "Total Hours to First Draft."

3. Determine How Many Outline Sections You Need to Complete

Take another look at your outline. It's likely that it consists of roughly three to seven major sections. Write that number down. Boom. Done. This part was easy.

However (it can never JUST be easy, can it?), some sections may take longer to write than others. So, take some time to evaluate the likely contents of each segment, then make a note of which sections are likely to take more and less time.

4. Find Your Daily/Per Session Time Target

Now for the serious (and seriously important) math. You're going to take your Total Hours to First Draft that you wrote down earlier, and divide it by the number of sessions you plan to write. If you are on a 5-week schedule as recommended in this book, and you plan to write each weekday, then you have 25 available sessions. If you plan to work in longer sessions on one weekend day each week, then you have 5 available sessions.

Let's take a look at this math in action.

If your Total Hours to First Draft is 35, and your available sessions are 25, then your daily target will be about 1 hour and 25 minutes (you can round up to 1.5 for a nice even number).

35 hours divided by 25 sessions = 1.4 hours per day (roughly 1 hour 25 minutes)

This is your Daily Time Target.

Finding Your Weekly Word Count Target

To get your weekly word count target, you're going to take your Manuscript Target Word Count and divide it by five, the target number of weeks to complete your first draft.

For example, if your target word count is 20,000 and your number of available days are 25, then your daily word target will be 800.

20,000 words divided by 25 days = 800 words a day

Remember that you are not going to hold yourself accountable to write 800 words EVERY day. Rather, it should average out over about a week. So next, take that 800 words and multiply it by the number of days per week you are writing. If you write 5 days a week, your weekly target will be 4,000 words.

20,000 words divided by 25 days = 800 words a day = multiplied by 5 = 4,000 words per week

This is your Weekly Word Count Target.

Finding Your Biweekly Outline Target

Finally, evenly distribute the number of outline sections you've created across the number of available weeks, making allowances for sections that may take more or less time to complete.

If you have seven outline sections of roughly equal length, and you have 5 available weeks, then you will want to complete roughly 1.4 outline sections each week. Multiply this by two to get your biweekly outline target, and you can see that you want to complete roughly 3 sections every two weeks.

7 outline sections divided by 5 weeks = 1.4 sections per week times 2 weeks = (roughly) 3 sections every two weeks

Whew. That was a lot of math. Oh, my head.

The hard part is done. I promise nothing else will hurt as much as the math (I'm lying; revisions are going to hurt more; but we can pretend).

Now, let's chart this out, based on our example:

- Per session time target: 1.5 hours
- Weekly word count target: 4,000 words
- Biweekly outline target: 3 sections

Got it? Now we're going to map the plan against your calendar and make it actionable!

Step Four: Review Your Calendar

Now you have a list of targets. Well done! You are much more organized than the vast majority of authors, and much more likely to complete your manuscript. Next up, let's take a look at your actual schedule.

What do you already have scheduled over the next 13 weeks? What holidays, vacations, or celebrations are coming up? Are there any big deadlines at work, or major tasks you need to complete? Realistically consider whether there are days or even weeks when you are unlikely to make any progress at all. It's much better to plan for this than to get surprised and discouraged by it later.

At the same time, notice any days or weeks when you will have a lot of open time that you would like to devote to your book.

Mark out the next five weeks that you're reasonably confident you can devote the amount of time you've set as your first draft target. Then mark out the two weeks after that for rest. Then mark out two good weeks after that when you can focus on revisions. Then the next two weeks for rest. And then another two weeks for editing.

Leave gaps in the writing plan for days and weeks when you already know you're unlikely to have a chance to work. You'll be much better off knowing these breaks are planned for, and much better able to get back on track when you come back.

Now sit back down with your calendar for the first five weeks, block out your first draft writing sessions. Inside each calendar event, make a note of the time target. On the last session event of each week, make a note of your weekly word count, so you can check against it. And at the last session of the second and fourth weeks, make a note of your outline section target, so you can check against that.

Each time you check in, re-evaluate your initial assumptions. Do you feel like your word count is still the right word count? Do you need to add or remove outline sections? Is it taking you longer to reach your word count than you thought?

Use this information to create a feedback loop and adjust your plan as you go, always with your eyes on the ultimate target.

Step Four: Plan for Revisions and Edits

You will mark up your calendar for the two weeks of revising and editing, as well, but you may want to do it differently. Especially during the revision period, you may find that you need larger blocks of time. Revising requires you to hold the full structure of your book in your head as you work through it, and that can mean it takes longer to get started at each session.

Most of the authors I work with prefer at least two-hour blocks for this part of the process.

Example: First draft targets for this book

- Estimated word count: 20,000
- Daily target: 1 hour per day, 5 days per week
- Weekly target: Roughly 4,000 words
- Biweekly target: Complete 4 chapters every two weeks

Chapter Six

REST STOPS
are the unsung heroes of
your creative process

If you follow blogs or read books about writing, very often you'll encounter over and over again the idea that if you want to write, you just need to write. Just do it. Just do it. Just do it.

I take issue with that. While I agree fundamentally that you have to put in the time to get the book done, the idea that you can just grind it out on willpower alone is dismissive of the reality of how our brains and bodies work. And I'm not here for the writer shame. Shame is a limiter, not a motivator.

There is much more to writing a book than sheer discipline.

The "just do it" advice, while well-meaning and sometimes helpful for some people, ignores the realities of human biology, psychology, and behavioral science. For the creative visionaries who write books, single-minded discipline is often counter-productive to the open-ended, free flow of ideas that is required to see new futures and unfold new ideas.

Successfully completing a manuscript is an alchemy of process *plus* creative flow. It is not just about getting ideas down on paper, but also allowing the much larger processes of your creative mind to arise and do magic on the page.

Why Rest Matters to the Creative Process

Under the surface of your busy brain is a bigger, more powerful part of you that notices everything, records everything, and processes everything, including a great deal that you are not consciously aware of. Think of it like an extra personal computer, running in the background, accessing the internet and processing it to complete tasks your conscious mind has (intentionally or unintentionally) set for it. Carl Jung calls this extra personal computer your unconscious mind, and it has access not only to everything you know and have experienced, but also a larger network called the collective unconscious.

The unconscious part of you requires time to receive, process, and integrate. Then it will reward you by sending you the best possible ideas. You already know this, because you've experienced it. Maybe it's that incredible idea you had this morning in the shower, something that came to you during meditation, or a problem you solved "miraculously" during a long drive.

This happens because you have given your brain a rest, and rest is the portal through which the unconscious mind speaks to us.

To get the most out of this process, you can set the unconscious mind "tasks." That's one of the secret (until now) reasons for your North Star Statement. You have very clearly set a focused task, and now your unconscious mind is actively working on it, even as you read these words. You've given it a mission, and it's on it. It'll come back with quest results in good time… if you give it a chance.

Additionally, rest allows your brain to prune away synapses that it no longer needs, and to strengthen connections that you have begun building. It works like muscles that have gotten a workout. If you work out every day at the gym on the same muscle groups over and over again, you will make less progress than if you allow your muscles to rest between workouts. During the rest time, your body strengthens and rebuilds tissues that were strained during the last workout.

Rest periods do the same thing for your brain and unconscious processes.

How to "Do" Rest

In our hyper-productivity focused culture, many of us have forgotten how to rest. It's a skill we must re-learn.

To begin, know that there are as many ways to "do" not doing as there are people. Resting doesn't have to mean lying in bed (but it can). It doesn't have to mean playing games (though it can!). If it doesn't feel restful to you, then it's not rest. The most important thing is to listen to yourself and give yourself the permission to rest in the ways that work best for you.

Here are some ideas to play with:

- **Sleep**. Take a nap. Choose not to set an alarm so you can sleep late.
- **Spend time in nature**. Forest bathing, ocean swimming, surfing, hiking, waterfall hunting, kayaking, camping–the great outdoors can be one of your best allies in the work of not working.
- **Binge your favorite shows or read books**. No guilt! Television, movies, poetry, plays, music, comic

books–these are all forms of art, and you are allowed to enjoy them. In fact, revel in them! But of course, read books too if you want to. You will learn as much about storytelling by consuming stories (in all forms) as you will by writing.

- **Have fun**. Go on dates, throw a party, play games with your kids, travel, start a new hobby, be extravagant. If money and time permit, why not go all out and do something you've always dreamed of but never given yourself permission to do?

- **Relax.** Get a massage or try a guided meditation. Soak in a hot bath or float in the ocean. Do something that gets your muscles to unwind and your mind to drift.

- **Find something else to work on**. If you really, really can't stand to "do nothing" you can still get the benefit of your rest period by focusing on something else. Try a new creative project, a new art form, or a remodeling project.

- **Go for a long drive**. Many people (myself included) find that driving provides just enough exercise for the brain to keep it active and awake, but plenty of freedom for the mind to wander and gather wool.

- **Just go on with life** however you normally do. Simply returning to your usual habits and daily life is a legitimate way to spend your rest time during the writing process. Remember, it's not what you are DOING that counts during this time. It's what you're NOT doing–which is working consciously and actively on your book.

Throughout this book, you will see signposts indicating that it's time to take a rest break. Take these breaks. They are not a cutesy suggestion, but rather an integral and critical part of the process, creating space for the vast underground network of your mind and heart to bring their own gifts to the process.

Exercise: Journal Entry

Time Estimate: 15-30 minutes

Resting: Such a simple concept. Yet most of us in this overheated productivity-addled culture struggle with it. So, to begin your unlearning of hyper-productivity and learning of rest, try this simple journaling exercise.

Find someplace you find peaceful. Maybe it's your patio or a hammock in the backyard, maybe it's your bed or a cozy corner of your library. Maybe it's someplace public like a park or a coffee shop. You decide what feels peaceful to you, and go there. Bring a pen and paper or other recording device.

Give yourself at least fifteen minutes for this exercise. Half an hour is better. Take a deep breath and allow your shoulders and face and hands to relax.

Hold the word "rest" in your head. Then start journaling. Use these questions to prompt your thoughts, but don't feel like you have to answer all of them. Just allow your thoughts to flow.

- What does rest mean to me?
- What are my favorite times and places to rest?
- How much rest do I actually get?
- What would feel restful to me right now?

- If I didn't have so many responsibilities, would I rest or would I feel like I need to be doing more things?
- Can I rest from one thing while doing another?
- Does this feel restful to me?
- Am I resting right now?
- When during my week can I build in routine periods of rest?

There are no right or wrong answers. The point of this exercise is not to discover the "correct" way to rest. It is to uncover for you your relationship with rest, and help you build a healthful relationship with the concept.

REST STOP

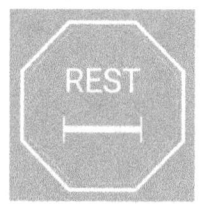

CHAPTER SEVEN

YOUR TECHNOLOGY
should streamline your journey

You can write a book almost anywhere that is available to you: On paper, in a word processor, on a tablet, or by voice recorder. Heck, my Uncle Pierce wrote a diary of his time as a POW in WWII on the back of can labels and toilet paper.

But some tools are easier than others (toilet paper isn't one of them).

In this section, I'll go over some of the best writing tools available at this time and show you how to set up your manuscript template.

How to Choose Your Software

Your software will define the experience you have while writing your book. The wrong software can create frustration and lead to loss of your work. The right software will make your process smoother and easier to navigate.

As of this writing, the primary software tools that most writers use for producing a manuscript are Google Docs, Microsoft Word, and Scrivener.

Of the three, at the time of this writing, I recommend Google Docs for nonfiction authors.

I've worked with dozens of authors across several decades, seen the rise and fall of as many platforms as there are years in my career. Google Docs is simply (currently) the easiest, cheapest, most secure, most flexible, and best collaborative platform for the purpose. And best of all, it's free.

Here's a brief comparison, so you can decide for yourself.

Microsoft Word

Microsoft Word is the standard platform in traditional editing, and you may at some point have to deliver a document in this format. But it has a lot of drawbacks, the biggest one being a lack of effective collaboration tools. The second biggest one being that it's expensive. It's cumbersome, top heavy, notoriously obstreperous, and it doesn't play nicely in the sandbox. You will sometimes need to deliver a draft in Microsoft Word format, but that is easily done by exporting from Google Docs.

Scrivener

Scrivener is a wonderful indy tool that I love dearly for fiction writing. It provides a lot of useful tools for plotting and managing your fiction manuscript. However, it lacks collaborative tools and is cumbersome for sharing and feedback. Plus, it's possible to lose older manuscripts simply because the formatting is no longer supported by Scrivener and you can't access Scrivener formatted documents from any other platform. It's also a little cumbersome to learn and has a lot of excess functionality that you won't use for creating non-fiction. Finally, exporting documents can create inconsistencies and complexities you don't need. I simply don't see it as a viable platform for anything other than drafting a fiction manuscript.

Google Docs

Google Docs is not perfect, but it is the best combination of collaborative, flexible, and practical available as of this writing. It provides all the essential tools you need to organize and develop a non-fiction manuscript, plus it's reliable, stable, and free to use. Its benefits:

- **Essential text-editing tools.** Superior built-in heading formats, plus all the standard editing tools.

- **Automatic outlining.** Apply built-in headings to your chapter headings, and then quickly and easily view and navigate your outline from within your draft. This becomes increasingly valuable as your draft grows long and complex. When formatted correctly, a Google Doc will let you see the structure of your draft in a panel to the side, and quickly navigate to any section with a click.

- **Autogenerated table of contents**. Long gone are the days when you had to painstakingly reorganize your table of contents every time you moved something around. By using the native heading formats inside Google Docs, you can autogenerate and auto-update your table of contents in a couple clicks.

- **Cloud-based collaboration**. Create your manuscript and immediately make it available to your feedback partners, editors, and other professionals. Cloud-based collaboration means you can share a "live" document so that you're all using one central document. No more multiple versions all over the place with no clear central "point of truth." Control who can do what in the draft, whether they can only view, only comment, or actually edit the draft.

- **The ability to track changes.** Dear gods, you MUST be able to TRACK the changes, especially when your feedback partners get into the document and start working. You do not want the nightmare of having to figure out what changes were made by whom.

- **Automatic versioning.** Google Docs backs up your work continuously in real time. This means that even if a feedback partner makes changes and forgets to track them, you can usually (usually!) recover the original and lose nothing. Plus, you can compare versions to see what changes have been made.

- **Back up your work anyway!** I recently lost an entire manuscript due to a mishap on my part and a corrupted file on Google's part. Luckily, I had a backup. Your manuscript is too valuable to take any chances on. I recommend routinely backing up to your hard drive, as well as sending updated copies to a trusted friend for safe keeping. (Ask them not to read it, but just to hang on to it: Too many cooks spoil a meal!)

How to Set Up Your Manuscript

At the start of the first draft process, I send my clients a Google Docs template and a video tutorial on how to set up the manuscript correctly from the start. If you're doing it yourself, here are the essential concepts you need to understand. Setting this up correctly will save you a lot of grief later, as the draft gets longer and longer and more difficult to navigate and organize.

1. Use native text styles to format your title, chapter, and subheadings.

Use the "Title" text format for the book's title. Use the "subtitle" format for the subtitle. Format your highest-level sections (chapter headings or "Part I" etc.) with the "Heading 1" format. Second-level sections (subsections of chapters, or chapters themselves if you're dividing the draft into larger "parts") format using "Heading 2". Then, "Heading 3" for the next level of subheadings, and so on. You can go as deep with subheadings as you like. In many cases, more detail is better. For this book, each "Part" was formatted in Heading 1, each "Chapter" is Heading 2, steps, subsections, and exercises are Heading 3, and so on.

2. Use the built-in "document outline" feature to navigate your document

When you use native text styles to format your document as described above, Google Docs automatically builds a document outline based on your formatting. Use the "show outline" feature to see your outline in real time as you build it. As of this writing and in the version I'm using in the Chrome browser on a MacBook, "show outline" can be found in the "View" menu. If you don't find it there, have a look around till you do. Once your outline view is showing, you can navigate to any portion of your draft simply by clicking on it in the outline view. This becomes a life saver as your manuscript grows in length.

Exercise: Set Up Your Manuscript

Use the guidelines in this chapter to set up a template for your manuscript by putting your working outline into a document and formatting the headings to show the outline while you work.

CHAPTER EIGHT:

YOUR PARKING LOT
is the secret to a smooth and uncluttered journey

Now that you've set everything else up, it's time to talk about one more essential tool you never knew you needed: Your parking lot.

The parking lot is an empty (at first) document where you dump everything you're not sure what to do with but think you might need later.

For now, all you need to do is open a new, blank document. Title it "Parking Lot - Draft Title," and leave it alone. As you work through the drafting and then the revising processes, use this document as a catch-all for content, ideas, cut material, notes, and anything else that you produce in your process and don't know what else to do with.

EXERCISE: CREATE YOUR PARKING LOT

That's it. It's that simple. This is probably the easiest step in the whole darn process. Enjoy it.

That said, you might already have some material to dump here. For instance, leftovers from your outlining process. Go ahead and "park" all that good stuff here, so you can clear your mind and move on.

REST STOP

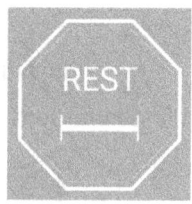

Part II

WRITE YOUR FIRST DRAFT
How to navigate the journey from blank page to first draft

I T'S GO TIME.

All your prep work is about to pay off, as you sit down to pound out the actual first draft of your book over the next few weeks. At this point, you may feel any number of emotions:

- Elation
- Anxiety
- Overwhelm
- Fear
- Excitement
- Determination
- Nothing at all - Numbness is not uncommon

Whatever you feel at the start, don't worry. It will change.

For better and worse.

In fact, your carefully assembled toolbox will change too. As Helmuth von Moltke once said, no plan survives first contact with the enemy. It's about to get messy.

During this stage, all those carefully developed bullet points, concepts, and ideas you organized in the planning stages start interacting with each other, develop minds of their own, and sometimes decide to do something entirely unhinged.

Don't let this stress you out. Messy is good. A first draft's only job is to exist, and you've got everything you need to make that happen.

During the course of writing, you will go through a huge range of emotions. Many of these emotions have the potential to stop you in your tracks, and prevent your beautiful gift of a book from ever being born into the world. The antidote? Just realize that it's all a normal part of the process.

THE
Creative Process

○ This is awesome!

○ This is tricky.

○ This is shit...

○ I am shit.

○ This might be okay...

○ This is awesome!

WORDS BY MARCUS ROMER, GRAPHIC BY FEN DRUADIN

This part of the book is designed to give you the tools, guidance, and understanding you need to successfully navigate the foggy path of the first draft process, and to get you unstuck when you get stuck. I got you!

Chapter Nine

FREE YOURSELF
to fill the page
(after page after page after page)

A re you ready to fill a blank page? Yes, no, maybe? Good news: You don't have to.

All the work you've done leading up to this moment means you don't have a blank page at all. You have a vision, a direction, an audience, an outline, and an execution plan.

The manuscript you've pre-populated with the tools you created in Part I is primed and ready for you to start filling it in.

But that doesn't mean the first draft journey won't be a bumpy one. It almost certainly will be. So, to help you out, here are four quick lessons that are going to make this part of the journey smoother.

Lesson One: Forget Perfection

Several years ago, I had the immense pleasure of standing in an auditorium and asking Saint Anne (I mean Anne Lamott, of course, author of *Bird by Bird*) one question.

My question?

"How do you keep writing when you're a constant ball of anxiety?"

Her answer: "I sit down and pat myself on the shoulder and say, 'There, there,' and then I write."

This seemingly simple advice has served me well. It reminds me:

- I don't have to be in a perfect state of mind to sit down and write.
- I don't have to feel confident in order to sit down and write.
- I can be kind and gentle with myself even when I'm a ball of anxiety.

Saint Anne is also responsible for the now-famous concept of the "shitty first draft."

The "shitty first draft" means: Don't worry about your first draft being good. A first draft's only job is to exist.

If it exists, it's a successful first draft.

Hold on to that like you're holding onto your hat on a rollercoaster. Because you just stepped onto a rollercoaster.

Whatever your goal for each day is, you're going to focus on getting there, not on getting there *perfectly*. Just… getting there. Progress, not perfection.

Lesson Two: Remember You Are Free

You don't have to write a book. You are choosing to write a book. You don't have to fill out your outline, you are choosing to fill out your outline (or not). And each session, when you sit down to write, you don't have to do anything you don't want to do. You are choosing to sit and write, but what you do during your writing time is up to you.

Be free.

You can write each section of your book in any order you want. You can move the outline around. You can go off on a tangent. You can write the ugliest, most horrible thing you ever wanted to say, right there on the page (don't worry, you can take it out later!).

For this round of writing, absolutely everything is fair game. For instance, you can:

- WRITE THE BOOK OUT OF ORDER. Jump around and write whichever part of the book feels good and fun and easy or just plain doable to you today. You can come back to the hard parts later, and they'll probably be less hard.

- FOLLOW YOUR FEELINGS. The other St. Anne (Anne Rice) once said that when writing, you should lean into your pain but also lean into your pleasure. Take that principle and use it to guide you each day in where to begin writing. Lean into whatever feels best or most urgent that day.

- PUT WORDS DOWN EVEN THOUGH THEY MAKE NO DAMN SENSE. If you're stuck, just go. Any movement is better than no movement. Write a bunch of garbage like, "I don't want to do this, I hate it, I hate Fen, why is Fen making me do this, I can't do it" (it's okay to blame me, I can take it) over and over until the dam breaks. It will break.

- WRITE WAY MORE THAN YOU'RE ACTUALLY GOING TO USE. Hemingway, bless his immortal sotted soul, advises that you "write it all in, then take most of it out." Your reader will know it was there, long after it's gone. This includes things you're afraid might hurt someone, get you in trouble, or break laws. Worry about that later (specifically, we'll address it in chapter 18–so you can release it for now). Right now, worry about getting the words down.

- COPY AND PASTE SOMETHING YOU WROTE ELSEWHERE. Many, many authors have already written portions of their book before they even knew they were going to write a book. It's fine to pull old blogs, articles, notes, and journal entries–anything you ever wrote, really–and simply paste them into your draft. It's fine if it doesn't flow quite right yet or if it will have to be rewritten. If the gist of it belongs somewhere in your outline, stick it there and carry on.
- INCLUDE OTHER PEOPLE'S WORK **BUT CAREFULLY**. If there's a point you want to make that someone else has also made, it's fine in your first draft to copy and paste portions of their work into your draft. BUT. Be VERY careful. The last thing you want is to get slapped for plagiarism because at some point you copied and pasted and later forgot it wasn't your own work (trust me, this does happen, and it's easier to do than you think). When you paste someone else's work into your work, clearly label it with the source so you can refer back to it later and ensure you're complying with fair use laws. Most professional copyeditors can help you navigate the waters of fair use, but you don't have to worry about it YET, as long as you're clearly marking other people's work within your draft.

- IGNORE YOUR TYPOS AND BAD GRAMMAR AND INCOHERENT SENTENCES. Seriously, *the only job your first draft has is to exist.* You don't have to be great at grammar or punctuation to be an author. You will revise and edit later, and editors will edit. Just get the words down.

- MAKE NO DAMN SENSE. You are probably more coherent than you realize, but if you feel incoherent some days, just write anyway. You can take it out or rewrite it later. Open the door to the possibility that your "incoherence" may contain more genius than you realize.

- DEPART FROM YOUR OUTLINE. Your working outline is a WORKING outline. It's not designed to be the final authority on what your book contains. Most authors find that their outline shifts a little or a lot over the course of writing the book. Don't stress about this. It is a tool to lean on, not a straitjacket to confine.

- STARE AT THE SCREEN or out the window, do-ing "nothing." As long as your butt is in the chair and you're focused on the book (not scrolling social media!) you're doing it. Your brain is very busy up there, even when it doesn't feel like it. Sometimes even more when it doesn't feel like it.

Embrace the fact of your freedom and allow your first draft to flow out of you, unimpeded by expectations about how the process "should" work. Just allow it to work.

Lesson Three: Embrace the Creative Heartspace

Creativity flows from relaxation and heart space. Allow yourself to relax before you sit down. Be comfortable. Have a lovely beverage by your side. Wear ear plugs or play relaxing music. Do whatever gets you into a "groove."

But don't be precious about it. Creativity also flows from the willingness to allow creativity to flow. Waiting on the perfect environment won't get you there. Commit to the activity, and then show up for the activity, and creativity will flow.

If you find yourself bogged down and stressed, take a minute. Stretch. Go for a walk. Get another nice beverage. Let your brain rest and consider moving to a different portion of the book, something that feels freer and easier.

If you're freaking out or procrastinating or doing everything in the world other than writing your book, just know that's totally normal. Just don't let yourself get stuck here. Check in with an accountability partner and check out chapter eleven for more on getting unstuck.

Make the space for your book to unfold, and then allow it to unfold.

Cheat Sheet: Things To Try When You're Stuck

- Breathe
- Set a timer and go for a brief walk
- Get another nice bevvie
- Review your outline and choose another place to work that feels less stuck
- Stare into the distance for five to ten minutes
- Don't give up
- Be gentle with yourself
- Check in with your book coach or accountability partner
- Fast forward to the Chapter Eleven for more on clearing blocks]

Lesson Four: Leave Yourself Breadcrumbs.

Writing a book is a large undertaking. At the start of each new writing session, you may find that it takes you a few minutes to get back into the groove. Over time, this transition period can start to feel demotivating.

You may waste time rereading to remember where you left off, struggling to pick up the threads of thought, or getting bogged down deciding what to work on next.

Do yourself a favor, and streamline the transition by leaving yourself breadcrumbs at the end of each session, to set yourself up for the beginning of the next.

There are a lot of ways to do this, but here's the method that works for me and for most of the authors I work with.

At the end of each session, leave a note inside the draft marking your place. Keep it simple. I use the words:

HERE HERE HERE

Then I use the built-in Heading 1 to make them stand out in the outline. When I sit down to write the next time, they're a big, bold signpost to where I left off.

Below the signpost, you can add brief instructions. For instance: "Write about breadcrumbs next," or "Do I need a section on rest periods?" Or "Go back and reread this section to see what's missing." I add these in normal text below the words "HERE HERE HERE."

You can do this directly in the document as I do, or you can keep a notebook for this purpose. If you use a notebook, it's a good idea to keep one just for this purpose, so you don't have to flip through lists and comments and diary entries to find it. Just make a note at the end of each session stating where you left off and what you want to work on next.

What you want to do next may be very explicit, such as write a particular section or develop a specific idea. Or it might be vague like "keep going." It might even be "Decide what to work on next." That's fine. Leave yourself that note. You'll save yourself a lot of brain power and time by not struggling to remember if you already had a plan or not and reminding yourself that "deciding what to work on next" is part of the work of writing a draft.

Exercise: Start Writing–Wooooooo!!!!!!

Time Estimate: 5 weeks

OMG IT'S GO TIME.

This chapter's exercise is simple: Just get some content into your draft. That's it. Choose a section to fill in and fill it in. With ANYTHING. And I do mean anything. Free yourself from expectation.

Read your North Star Statement, review your outline, and then just GO.

Start anywhere. Do anything, as long as it's getting words into your document.

Cut material from something else you wrote and paste it in, even if it only kind of fits. Free write from your heart, whatever comes to mind. Create a chart to explain a key idea. Write a poignant story. Make a list. Daydream onto the page. Transcribe a conversation.

Just do it, put it where it seems to make sense right now, and keep going till you've filled up your allotted time for the session.

Show up for your sessions, check in on your targets, embrace your freedom, and keep going. That's it. That's all you have to do.

One last thing. At some point, you will get stuck. It is inevitable. But do not fear! It just means you're ready for Chapter Ten.

AVOID COMMON TRAPS
that can stall your journey

When we give ourselves space to freely explore and express our thoughts, the first draft process flows more smoothly. But you're still going to hit bumps. Here are four common traps that can catch you up and slow you down. Learn to recognize them and move past them and you'll get to the end much faster.

Four Common Author Traps

1. The research rabbit hole trap
2. The new project trap
3. The "let me just perfect this bit" trap
4. The "I forgot what I'm doing" trap]

The Research Rabbit Hole Trap

Many people who feel called to write a book do so because we have a lot of expertise to share with the world, and a unique perspective that enables us to help people see the world in new ways.

Often, this expertise and perspective is accompanied by and (partially) fueled by an obsession with research.

Research may have gotten us here, but it won't get us to the finish line.

While a certain amount of research is a normal part of the process of writing a book, it can become a trap that stops you from making progress.

Pay attention to how often you stop writing to "just check something real quick" and end up down an hours-long rabbit hole pursuing interesting information that may or may not be important for your book.

Pay attention to how often you start thinking that you can't keep writing until you know more about a topic that you don't know a lot about.

Then remember: You got to this point in the journey because you know things.

Everything you need is inside you already.

Is research valuable? Yes, of course. And there is a place for books that are thoroughly researched and documented.

We need academics and researchers publishing information based on research.

But *this* book, the one you are working on right now, doesn't have to be that. Most books aren't. You probably know more about every subject you're writing about than you realize.

Sometimes, research rabbit holes are a device your subconscious mind uses to distract you from the fact that you're afraid or anxious about completing your book.

If you find yourself down one of these rabbit holes, flip forward to chapter eleven. Our emotions are usually at the root of the ways we undermine ourselves, and the tools in that chapter will help you move through and beyond what's stopping you.

The New Project Trap

Another trick our subconscious minds use to stop us from completing THIS project is to remind us of THAT project we always wanted to do. Or to give us middle-of-the-night visions of a ground-breaking idea that we just absolutely must pursue because it is going to change our lives.

Most people who are feral enough to write a book are at least a little distractible, too.

You may have unfinished projects piled up all over your house–paintings, sewing projects, knitting, whittling, home improvement, basket weaving (guilty).

You may have unfinished manuscripts piled up all over, too (guilty on all counts).

First things first: Don't beat yourself up about this.

Be kind to you.

Unfinished projects are the sign of an active mind and ambitious heart. I, myself, have SEVERAL manuscripts for other books sitting on the same drive this draft is sitting on, and I, in this exact moment, am seriously contemplating returning to another one instead of finishing this one because…that would be a very good way of tricking myself into believing that I'm being productive when actually what I'm doing is avoiding completing the project right in front of me.

I do want to add a caveat which is that being distracted by another project can be productive, if it leads to completing that project. But if your goal is to finish *this* book, and you find yourself continually distracted by other projects, it's time to make a commitment to stick with this one. After all, it's only five weeks. Then you can go get distracted by something else.

To get yourself out of the "new project trap," take a look at your North Star Statement. THAT is what you are doing and WHY. Take a minute to envision the world you're creating with your book. Let that motivate you.

If you need more help, hire an accountability partner to help you stay on track. *Paying* someone to help you stay on track can be very effective, as our minds have a tendency to prioritize what we pay for.

Also, remember that subconscious emotions are 95% of what drives the behaviors we can't seem to stop. So jump to chapter eleven and try it out.

Finally, just know that staying focused on this project doesn't have to mean you never get to the other projects. Give yourself a moment to make a note of new ideas that come to you, and keep a list of them in another document. This tells your brain that you are not ignoring it, that you value all these great new ideas, and that you will make space for them: After you finish this draft.

The "Let Me Just Perfect This Bit" Trap

It is a rare author who can perfect their writing as they go and still complete the draft. Anne Rice was one such author, rest her beautiful soul.

But for the rest of us mere mortals, the urge to make each section perfect before we move to the next can be a bottomless pit. Yet another way our subconscious tricks us into thinking we're being productive when we're actually avoiding completing the project.

It's okay to go back and review your work when it helps you. If you like to reread the section from the previous day before getting started, and that helps motivate you for today's work, then by all means do that.

If you see that parts of it could be better, go ahead and spend a little time improving them.

But pay attention when you start to feel stuck. If you're spending large portions of your daily writing time on making previous sections better, and not adding much to your word count, then your desire for perfection is holding you back.

Remember that this is just a first draft. *Its only job is to exist.* Its only job is to exist. Just get the words down so you can work with them later. And if you need help getting unstuck…chapter eleven.

The "I Forgot What I'm Doing" Trap

Occasionally, our minds decide to take us on a lovely ramble through the countryside to enjoy the scenery…scenery that has nothing to do with the particular journey we're on. The journey of THIS book.

There is a fine line between just getting your first draft down with whatever comes to mind, and getting distracted by starting to write a different book within the same document.

This is the "I forgot what I'm doing so I'm going to do something else entirely" trap.

To avoid this trap, start each writing session by reviewing your North Star Statement. When it feels right, look at your outline as well to orient yourself to the work before you dive in. For extra help, a book midwife like me can help you discern whether what you're dumping into the draft is true to the vision or just a distraction.

If you do find yourself ambling down a pleasant lane lined with horse pastures and stands of oak and pecan trees, with mountains fading in the distance against the horizon, miles and miles from where you meant to be today…well, no worries. A lovely afternoon jaunt never did anyone any harm.

Now grab that beautiful piece of prose you just laid down, and put it in your parking lot for later. And get back to work!

But if those afternoon jaunts start to take over…guess what? Chapter eleven.

EXERCISE: FAVORITE TRAPS INVENTORY

Time Estimate: 15 minutes

Take a moment to reflect on your past experiences with projects you've started and then stopped. What are your favorite ways to procrastinate and avoid completing the work? Identify them and make a list.

Do any of them fit the categories in this book? Have you invented entirely NEW categories of procrastination traps? Clever you! Place the list near where you work. When you find yourself "stuck," take a look at your list, and remind yourself that you are in control. Revisit the relevant section of this book, call your book midwife, do the exercises in chapter eleven, and get yourself moving forward again.

CLEAR BLOCKS with Root 11

If there is one experience almost all writers share in common, it's the experience of writer's block. Whether you are just sitting down to write for the first time, halfway through a rough draft, or partway into a fifteenth round of revisions on your manuscript, there will be times when you just can't seem to make yourself do the thing.

"People who deny the existence of dragons are often eaten by dragons. From within."

~ Ursula K. Le Guin

One of the most pernicious aspects of writer's block is that it very often shows up in disguise. It can look like:

- Procrastination
- A sudden need to clean the house
- The conviction that your project is garbage and you might as well quit now

- The certainty that a different project is actually more important
- "Laziness"
- An ill-defined sense of "something not right"
- Exhaustion
- Lack of motivation
- Frustration
- Boredom
- Irritability
- Distractibility
- Shut-down
- And so on

Other times, it can show up very directly as fear, anxiety, or even just a blank mind. Or, you might physically experience writer's block as a lump in your throat or an ache in your back. You might even have a full-blown panic attack.

Writer's block is the #1 reason why books don't get finished. But it doesn't have to stop you from finishing yours. In fact, I'm about to let you in on an important secret:

All writer's blocks (and other creative blockages) are caused by the same thing, and can be cleared in the same way.

Bold claim, I know. But my work with hundreds of authors confirms: Root 11 is your "route" through and past writer's block.

What Is Root 11?

Root 11 is a guided process I developed that clears out creative blocks once and for all by identifying the internal misalignment at its root, and facilitating a conversation that enables a gentle realignment and integration process to take place. This integration, once complete, is permanent. Once a block is cleared, it's gone forever. And the best news? Clearing your creative blocks in this way has major implications for the rest of your life as well.

Think of it this way. If you're driving a car and one of your wheels goes out of alignment, it's going to cause all kinds of havoc. Even a small misalignment will cause your car to wobble, pull one direction or the other, and guzzle gas. Eventually, it may cause the car to stop operating altogether, because one part of the car wants to go in a different direction from the other parts.

Writer's block is exactly like this. Inside ourselves are many parts. Some of the parts of ourselves are conscious, and some live below the level of consciousness. If you're writing a book, at least some of you wants to write a book. If you have writer's block, at least some of you doesn't.

This is the misalignment.

Root 11 is the process by which you identify the part of you that is working against your best interests, and have a gentle conversation that results in recruiting that part of you to agree with your best interests and work with you instead of against you. That's the realignment and integration.

Why is it called Root 11?

What do you think of when you hear "Root 11"? Most people think immediately of a road, like Route 66. That's not an accident. Root 11 is a road, it's a clear path from stuckness back into the flow of creativity.

But it's spelled "root" because the process involves going straight to the root of the problem. The word "root" also refers to the root chakra. If you're familiar with the symbology of numbers, you'll recognize that the number 11 symbolizes awareness and your higher power: In other words, it's associated with the crown chakra.

One of the ways that creative blocks manifest is in your energy field, that is, your chakras. They can block the proper flow of energy from root to crown and back again. Root 11 clears these blocks so that energy can flow properly from root to crown.

But wait, that's not all! The number 11 also represents alignment. It's two lines next to each other,

---

which visually resemble a straight path or a road. (We're back to route 11!) So you can think of Root 11 as going to the root of the misalignment, and moving it back into alignment, so you have a clear path forward.

Finally, the number 11 also can represent insight and creative flow, associated with the sixth (third eye) and second (sacral) chakras respectively. These two energy centers in the body are critical powerhouses fueling and guiding the creative process. And guess what? Root 11 helps get them cleared out, powered up, in line, and shining bright.

Root 11. That's what's up.

The Theoretical Basis of Root 11

If you just want to get right to it, you can skip to the next section. But if you want to understand the theoretical basis of the work you're about to do, here it is.

1. Almost all writing blocks are caused by emotions. Often, these emotions exist below the level of consciousness.

2. All emotions live inside our bodies and represent a part of the self.

3. All the parts of the self have important roles to play. Misaligned parts simply misunderstand their role, often due to trauma, limiting self beliefs, coping mechanisms that no longer serve us, and internalized social conditioning.

4. We can locate the emotion that is causing a block within the body, and have a conversation with the part of ourselves that it represents.

5. This conversation enables us to understand the role that that part of us is playing, and the needs that it is advocating for.

6. This conversation can help that part of ourselves to uncover and claim for itself a healthier role within us that is supportive of our creative process.

7. Through this conversation, we "recruit" that part to join the "team" and help us rather than prevent us from achieving our shared goals.

I developed Root 11 over many years of working with clients and decades of study, practice and implementation of a wide range of psychological, somatic, and spiritual teachings. Root 11 is grounded in both modern modalities and ancient spiritual traditions including:

1. Guided meditation

2. Somatic theory

3. Parts theory and Internal Family Systems (IFS)

4. Jungian shadow work

5. Other forms of energy, chakra, and intuitive work, as well as my trained gifts as a seer and oracle

6. Earth-based knowledge and magic

6. Flow theory

How to Clear Blocks with Root 11

The first key to clearing writer's block, is to start paying attention to your creative process and noticing when you start to slow down or feel stuck. Sometimes you just need a little break or to work on a different part of your draft. But if the slow-down and stuckness continue past one or two writing sessions, it's time to try Root 11.

Step One: Notice Resistance

Think of the process of writing your book as a process of flowing, like a river running down to the ocean.

It may hit snags and branches and boulders, it may slow down in some places or fall precipitously over the edge in others. But it always flows, flows, flows down toward its destination.

When you are in this state of "flow", everything in your being works together toward a singular goal.

Flow is an actual, measurable psychological state originally identified by the Czech psychologist Mihaly Csikszentmihalyi (roughly pronounced Mi-ha-lee-yay Chi-chen-mi-ha-lee-yay). Later, Stephen Kotler and others studied and expanded our understanding of the state, creating practices and methods for harnessing its power.

If you want to learn more about the biological drivers of "flow" and how to stack them for extraordinary performance, try Kotler's book, *The Art of Impossible*.

What you need to know about flow for now is that it can be impeded by emotions and thoughts in our subconscious that we may not be immediately aware of.

When this happens, you are likely to experience a state of "resistance." This can show up in all the ways I described earlier, as procrastination or distraction and so on. But it originates from inside you, from an internal desire to "not do the thing"–wherein "the thing," in this case, is to write your book.

The first step in moving past the resistance is to simply notice when it's happening.

Then accept that it is happening, and flow into the next step.

Step Two: Pause to Feel the Resistance

When we feel resistance, our usual automatic response is to want to push past it right away.

This can work in the short term, but it uses up valuable energy and eventually those hidden emotions that are causing the resistance build up like sticks and leaves in a stream and clog our ability to flow.

So your next step is to pause and actually allow yourself to feel the resistance.

When you give yourself a moment to feel the resistance, you give yourself the space you need to start working with it instead of pushing against it.

Think of that leaf in a stream of water that has lodged itself against a branch that is stuck against a rock.

If the leaf wants to continue to flow, it can't do it by continuing to push against the branch that's lodged against the rock. The rock is too big and too heavy and the leaf is too stuck.

Imagine the same leaf is provided with a reprieve. A brief break in the flow of the water allows it to rest and back up.

Allowed to flow backward for a moment, the leaf can "breathe"–and possibly find a way to flow around the obstacle and continue on its way.

Your pause to allow yourself to recognize and feel the resistance is like that breath.

And now, you're ready for step three.

Step Three: Identify the Emotion In Your Body

Take a moment to tune into your body.

As soon as you stopped to feel your resistance, you may have noticed some things happening in your body.

Tension.

Pain.

Shortness of breath.

Tightness in shoulders or neck.

Pressure behind the eyes.

We like to think of our bodies and minds as separate things, but the brain is a part of the body–and the body is a part of the brain. What happens in one part, happens in the other parts.

What you're feeling in your emotions will always show up in your body. Most of the time, we ignore this connection, to our detriment. Take a moment to feel where in your body resistance is showing up for you right now.

Can you identify or name the emotion behind that resistance? It may be fear, but it may be something else. Go ahead and name it if you can, but if you're not sure, it's okay to move forward without a name for it, as long as you've identified where in your body you're experiencing it.

Step Four: Have A Conversation With Your Part

Now that you've identified your emotion and where it's living in your body, it's time to have a conversation.

Caution: The next part of this exercise may potentially generate some discomfort and anxiety for you. This is completely normal. However, it should not be painful or overwhelming. If the sensations you experience become overwhelmingly intense, you can stop at any time and breathe and remind yourself of where you are. Seek licensed mental health assistance if negative feelings linger or interfere with your daily life.

Take a few moments to relax and calm yourself. Sit or lie down in a comfortable position.

Take a deep breath in, then let it out.

Close your eyes.

Breathe in again, and then out, and this time, allow yourself to relax as you breathe out.

Repeat several times. Each time, allow more tension to flow out of your body with each breath. Notice your shoulders relax, your back, your toes, your arms, your face, the muscles in your scalp. Each time, allow more and more tension to flow out from different parts of your body.

When you are feeling relaxed, feel into your body for the emotion you identified earlier. Where is it living in your body?

At this point, it's important to let go of your critical thinking and not worry about whether what you experience makes logical sense. It may not make any sense to you at all. That's okay.

We're working with a part of the consciousness that is not ruled by the logical brain. Allow yourself to experience exactly what you're experiencing, without judgment. We'll make sense of it later.

Take your attention to the place in your body where the feeling is most intense.

What does it feel like in your body?

Does it have a shape?

A color?

Is it making a sound?

Does it have a texture?

Is it static or does it move around?

Does it have weight?

Is it hot? Cold?

You may experience it in multiple parts of your body and in multiple ways. There's no need to judge your experience. Simply feel what you're feeling and allow it to be what it is.

When you've spent some time with the feeling, take another deep breath and see if you can bring your awareness and attention down to the place in your body where the feeling is living. If it's in multiple places, follow it to the place where it feels most intense or where you feel called to pursue it.

Imagine you're approaching this place in your body as if you were approaching a wild animal that you are interested in getting to know. Be gentle and kind, even if it seems a little aggressive or painful.

Just sit with it. And when you've sat with it for a little while, you can gently begin to have a conversation with it. Here are some questions you may wish to ask it:

- Who are you?
- What would you like to tell me?
- What would you like to know from me?
- Do you have any gifts you want to give me?
- How can I help you?

You may find that the feeling shifts and changes as the conversation continues. Often, our challenging feelings simply want to be seen and heard and allowed, and then they are ready to be integrated. Other times, they have messages for us that will help us along the way. Or, they may want us to do something that will help them to feel safe so that they can begin to work with us instead of against us.

It's important to understand that every part of us is doing the best it can with what it has. Listen with openness and compassion, even if you disagree with what it is saying.

You may be surprised or even confused by what you hear and experience when you do this exercise. It's okay not to understand it at first. Just listen and be present for the experience.

Notice how the feeling shifts as you have the conversation. Does the color change, the texture, or the hardness?

Many people find that the feeling in their body softens as they have this conversation.

Or the feeling may shift to somewhere else in the body.

Sometimes, the feeling and its resistance may harden and strengthen, as the part feels threatened by your approach. Go gently, and allow it to feel what it feels. Listen and assure it that you're not asking it to stop, that in fact you want to understand and honor it.

It's okay to shift your attention, too, and to have a conversation with other places in your body, or to bring yourself back to full consciousness to process what's happened so far, and then return later if you like.

As you move your attention to different places in your body, take a moment to express gratitude to each part of yourself. Gratitude is a critical part of this work.

Be very gentle with yourself and with the parts of yourself that you're talking to.

However difficult they may feel, these are all parts of you that want to be heard and want to help you if you'll let them.

At some point, you will feel the energy inside yourself shift, and a sense of readiness for the misaligned part of yourself to assume a new role and to work with you in a more healthful and supportive way.

When this occurs, you may feel tears, chills, or a sense of lightness. You may experience relief, excitement, pleasure, or delight. You will feel immediately clearer than you did before.

At this point, be sure to take a moment to recognize the transition, and to express gratitude to the part of yourself that has done this work, and gratitude to your greater self for being willing to have this conversation.

When you feel complete, allow yourself to gently return your consciousness to where you are.

Feel the chair or mat or bed beneath you. Wiggle your toes. Stretch your fingers. Take a good breath. Open your eyes.

Give yourself a few minutes to reflect on what you experienced. If you're working with a professional, share as much detail as you can and allow them to help you interpret and understand the experience.

When the process is complete, you will experience a new level of integration between your body, emotions, unconscious mind, conscious mind and your energetic or spiritual self. You may feel this as lightness, brightness, clarity, inspiration, or simply being energized and ready to flow.

Go ahead at this time and follow your desires, whether you want to rest and integrate, or get moving on your draft again immediately.

Step Five: Enjoy the Relief of Innate Motivation and Inspiration

In my many years of developing and delivering Root 11, my clients almost universally experience relief, calm, and a sense of innate motivation as a result.

Jane found fear rising in her one day when she sat down to write, and immediately contacted me. We scheduled a session, and I guided her through Root 11. She discovered fear in her throat, presenting itself as a thick clot of green goo. During the conversation with it, it told her that it was afraid of her succeeding and actually having the book out there where others would read it.

This was a revelation to her! Fear of succeeding? Who would have thought?

In fact, it's a very common fear that most of us are unconscious of. Once Jane became aware of this fear, she was able to reassure herself that she would be okay. That she could mitigate the real dangers of having a book published (for instance, potential liability and/or people in her life reading about themselves in unflattering ways), and relieve herself of the unrealistic ones.

She felt the green goo soften and then evaporate. Her throat was clear of obstruction!

Following our twenty-minute session, she immediately went back to work on the draft and never had trouble with it again.

Justin felt blocked before he even spoke to me the first time. He had a book idea he was excited about, but a different idea felt more important, but also boring. He didn't feel like he could pursue the exciting project until he slogged his way through the other one. After a brief conversation, we determined that the idea he was passionate about was also the most important and impactful book he could write, and therefore the right place to focus his attention. But he still felt resistance.

I guided him through Root 11. He discovered a wall inside himself, stiff and rigid, dividing him in half at his solar plexus, preventing his lower chakras from communicating with his upper chakras. Through a conversation, he discovered that this part of him was protecting him from dangers he had been socialized to believe would occur if he accessed his primal creative centers.

This wall had formed during childhood, and it did not want to leave, nor did we ask it to. Instead, we focused on understanding the purpose it was serving and the needs it was fulfilling. Through discussion, we allowed it to uncover for itself the realization that it did not need to protect him from himself, because there was nothing inside himself that was dangerous. Furthermore, it discovered for itself a higher purpose of providing a shield from the ugly things that outsiders might say about Justin. Justin physically felt the wall lift and shift forward, and form itself on the outer edge of his energy field, protecting his inner sacred space and opening up the flow between his chakras.

Following this session, he was able to immediately get on board to pursue the exciting project he'd been dreaming of for many years, and to begin the drafting process.

One of my clients, Katrina, was so moved by her experience with Root 11 that she wrote about it in her book, *A Million Reasons Why You Can't*. In a chapter titled "I Meet My Shrill Librarian," she recounts how she met a part of herself that was intent on "shushing" her, keeping her quiet to protect her from criticism, and how she learned to invite the "shrill librarian" in to help her out.

The details of each person's experience with Root 11 is entirely unique, and often vastly different from anyone else's. Every time I guide a client along Root 11, I enjoy discovering what delightful, creative, and interesting forms their various protective parts take. Sometimes these parts can be pretty strong-willed or even rather scary. Always, eventually, they do reveal their essential protective, loving nature, and become willing to move into alignment.

I get chills when they reach that moment of transformation, when the protective part discovers a new role that moves it into a joyful flow and ease with the rest of the self.

I use Root 11 on myself, as well, and not just for creative blocks: it's useful for processing any difficult "stuckness" you may experience in life. Once you have cleared a block with Root 11, that block is gone forever. But if you, like most of us, have lots of parts of the self that work against you, you may benefit from multiple Root 11 sessions to gradually bring them all into alignment. Additionally, life can throw us curve balls that can cause new misalignments, sort of like driving your car over a curb too hard can cause your wheels to go wonky. Root 11 is an excellent routine practice to keep your chakras lined up and shiny and your full self actualized and standing in your power.

Cautionary Note: When Difficult Feelings Arise

While most people experience enormous relief through this practice, it can sometimes bring up feelings and emotions that are difficult to manage, especially if you have repressed a great deal throughout your life. When this happens, that doesn't mean the process *caused* the difficult feelings. It means that you have stored something in your body that is bigger than a few Root 11 sessions can address.

Most likely, you have stored trauma, whether you're aware of it or not.

It's important to seek professional help, whether with a licensed professional therapist or any number of trauma-informed alternative therapies.

You may also find reading about trauma and shadow work to be useful.

I highly recommend Janet Barrett's book *Stop the Break* for a practical, down-to-earth guide to understanding trauma and developing a life-long practice to heal, maintain, and thrive.

For a highly effective (and actually fun!) approach to shadow work, I recommend Carolyn Lovewell (formerly Elliott)'s excellent and more-than-a-little "naughty" *Existential Kink*.

Exercise: Try Root 11

Time Estimate: 20 to 45 minutes

Use the instructions in this chapter to explore a difficult emotion you are experiencing or have recently experienced. To experience the full power of Root 11 with a skilled practitioner, you can book a personal guided session by contacting me through my website at fendruadin.com.

CHAPTER TWELVE:

SH*T HAPPENS
but it doesn't have to stink up
the whole journey

Life has this weird habit of just…happening. Often when we least expect it and it's most inconvenient.

The car breaks down and needs expensive repairs. A kid is struggling at school and needs interventions. A grandparent falls ill. A friend dies. A sudden opportunity to go to Barcelona arises.

One year, I was planning to take a deep-dive class with a spiritual teacher I'd been following. A friend told me to be aware that when I began down that path, it was likely to turn my life upside down and inside out.

I decided that I had too much to do to bother with having my life turned upside down just now, thankyouverymuch.

I contacted the teacher and said that I was going to wait and join the path when I was feeling a little more able to cope with disruption.

One week later, my wife let me know that our marriage was over.

The spiritual call had come in, I had said yes, and the universe was not letting me off the hook.

My life turned upside down, whether I felt ready for it or not.

I did eventually finish that course of study. I learned the hard way that a contract with Spirit is not one to be broken lightly, and I've been more mindful since.

Writing a book is a spiritual journey, and life has a way of delivering lessons we didn't realize we needed. Sometimes it feels like the universe is testing us, just to see: Are you actually committed to writing this book? Despite everything?

So let's talk about what happens when life throws you a curveball in the middle of your writing process.

It's okay to set your goals aside for a day or two or even a week or longer, depending on the size of the disruption. Let yourself off the hook. Then, when you can, check in on your writing plan and adjust it to course correct for the disruption.

One of my authors found himself sidetracked by a major celebration in his daughter's life that he'd forgotten to plan for. We reworked his timeline to give him a break that week, and then he was right back on track. Another author lost her job and became the target of an online hate campaign plus multiple lawsuits all at once. We encouraged her to take a break until life becomes a little less…life-y.

Almost everyone experiences some level of disruption at some point. That's okay. Just don't let it turn into self-blame, and don't let it derail you permanently.

If you're like me, maybe you have bursts of super productivity followed by days or even a week of "crashes." I have learned to simply accept the crashes and know that I will come out the other side with a burst of productivity to make up for it.

I build in "crash days" and plenty of rest time, to reduce the number of crashes I have, and so that when they do occur, I have the space to flow with it.

One last tip: When the life-y life stuff happens and you decide to take a break to deal with it, try to find a moment to leave yourself some extra breadcrumbs (see chapter nine). That way, when you get back on track, it's easy to jump right back in again.

EXERCISE: PLAN FOR SELF-CARE

Time Estimate: 15 minutes

They say when the going gets tough, the tough get going. But you don't have to be tough to write a book. In fact, I don't recommend it. Softness, a willingness to allow the world in, to be changed, to be moved, to be touched by the things we experience–these are essential ingredients for the author.

And those qualities don't always play well with "tough."

So, instead: When the going gets tough, go easy.

Be the leaf in the stream and allow the flow to take you backward from time to time, so you can flow forward again.

Your assignment: Make a self-care plan now, so when life goes sideways, you don't have to go with it.

1. List ten to twenty things that feel comforting and/or enjoyable to you.

2. Block time in your calendar and do one or more of them regularly as routine self-care maintenance.

3. Keep the list handy, and use it to fuel your self-care during tough times.

4. Lather, rinse, repeat until the book is done (and beyond).

Interlude: How to Know When You're Done

At some point it's going to happen: Your first draft is complete.

But... what exactly does that mean? You'd be surprised how many authors struggle with knowing when it's time to call it "done" and hand it off to the developmental editor.

Common questions authors ask me as they close in toward that first draft completion: What if I missed some parts? What if my conclusion doesn't sound right? What if I'm sure the whole thing is garbage and I need to start over???

Don't worry, I got you. All you need to know is the answers to these four questions:

1. Does the draft exist?
2. Does it have words in it?
3. Does it say most of what I wanted to say?
4. Do I FEEL like it's *mostly* done?

If you can answer "yes" to three out of the four, then you're done. Make a backup copy, and hand that baby off to your developmental editor.

CHAPTER THIRTEEN:

YOUR FIRST DRAFT IS DONE…
Now what???

O h, wait, what? A COMPLETED draft? How did that happen?

If you continue along the path outlined in this book, eventually it's going to happen. Maybe faster than you dreamed. Authors who work with me consistently complete their first drafts in roughly five weeks. And then it's done.

So…what then?

Well, first of all, expect some weird-as-heck feelings to arise. This happens to almost everyone. After all, producing a full draft is a huge undertaking, one you may have been wanting for years or decades, and now it's done. It's a shock to the system.

You may think that you'll feel nothing but elation, but elation is often *not* the first thing folks feel. It's almost never what I feel.

When I get to the end of a first draft, I sit and stare at it in disbelief.

I feel numb.

You'd think I'd feel happy, but I almost never do. Not at first.

I JUST WROTE A BOOK DAMMIT ISN'T IT SUPPOSED TO FEEL GOOD??????

I can't say what you will feel when you finish that first draft. Maybe you're one of the lucky ones that actually ENJOYS BEING DONE and FEELS A SENSE OF ACCOMPLISHMENT.

Maybe you have a properly functioning dopamine system. Lucky you.

But maybe you'll feel something else. Something like:

Frantic

Afraid

Stunned

Proud

Weird

Embarrassed

Surprised

Numb

Here's the thing. Whatever you feel, it's okay. Emotions are wild animals, not to be tamed. Allow yourself a moment or a day to process.

This is huge.

You have done a HUGE thing.

Breathe.

If you haven't already, make a backup copy and send another backup to a very highly trusted dear friend for safe keeping. Tell them under pain of death not to open it. Only your developmental editor is allowed to look at it right now. See sidebar for why.

If you are uncomfortable with your emotions right now, use the first couple steps in chapter eleven to check in with yourself.

Check in with your support system so they can help you move into a celebratory mood.

Call your book midwife. (I promise they want to know and celebrate with you!) Call your mom. Dad. Kids. Bestie. Writing coach. Book club. Whoever will be the most excited for you and not demand to read the draft.

Post about your accomplishment on social media if you want.

Then actually go celebrate. DO SOMETHING FUN.

It's TIME FOR A BREAK.

Protect The Vision

At this stage of the process, it may be tempting to share your work with your friends and trusted associates. I encourage you to resist this urge.

Think of your vision for your book like a seed in the soil. You spent so much time cultivating the soil, turning it over and prepping it with nutrients, selecting your seed, placing it at just the right depth, and watering it gently. You wouldn't invite someone over to dig up the soil and look at your seed before it was ready, right? And even after the sprouts start showing, you wouldn't invite mean old Aunt Mildred over who never likes anything you do, to critique your garden layout, right?

It's the same.

When it comes to sharing early drafts of your book, choose your who and your when very carefully.

In other words: SEVERELY limit who reads your first draft. Protect the vision.

If your draft does end up in the wrong hands somehow, remember St. Anne Rice. In a YouTube video, she gave some of the best writing advice I've ever heard (paraphrasing):

"Don't take criticism from someone who hates your book. If they hate it, they don't get it. Only take feedback from people who love and understand your book."

Don't hand your precious little baby (ahem, book) off to Aunt Mildred.

Or anyone else (except your editor), for that matter. Even well-meaning advice, too soon, can spoil the pudding. There will be a time and place for sharing with a select group of trusted individuals, but this is not it.

EXERCISE: REST

Time Estimate: Two weeks

That's it. That's the whole exercise. Take a break and do something fun. Give yourself at least two weeks.

REST STOP

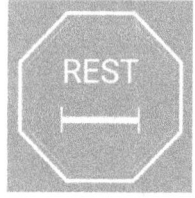

PART III

SHAPE YOUR MANUSCRIPT
How to turn your messy first draft into a publication-ready manuscript

Whoa. You wrote a whole book. Sure, it's in rough form right now, but it's all there. Your book. It's alive.

Whether it's your first book or your fiftieth, it's huge to finally have that book-length draft complete.

Now, it's time to take it from messy draft to complete fulfillment of the vision you have for it. This is going to happen in two main steps: Revising and editing. These correspond to two types of feedback you'll want from a professional editor: Developmental editing and structural editing (see sidebar).

If you compare creating a manuscript to whittling a wooden sculpture, the first draft is like cutting out the rough form of the wood quickly, perhaps with a power tool. You just want it close enough to work with. Think chainsaw sculpture, and you're just getting the basic form.

Revising is like taking a handsaw and refining the overall form of the wood to look more like what you originally envisioned.

Editing is like using a carving knife and rough grade sandpaper to take off the rough edges and refine the wood to look the way you want.

When those steps are complete, you'll hand it off to copyeditors and proofreaders. These are like the final polish with a very fine grain of sandpaper and some finishing oil.

There may be plenty of extra rounds in each step, and that's normal too.

The first draft was hard to write, but you did it. Well, I have bad news. Revising is *harder*.

In fact, the vast majority of authors I work with agree that the first round of revisions is the hardest part of all. Somehow, you've got to hold an entire book-length messy first draft in your mind, and know how to shape it into a final manuscript.

The good news: You don't have to go it alone. That's what this part of the book is for.

Even better news? Subsequent rounds of revision and editing tend to get easier and easier.

Let's begin.

CHAPTER FOURTEEN

THESE FOUR TYPES OF EDITING
are the key to a polished final manuscript

When most people think of editing, they think of someone to correct their grammatical mistakes. But professional editing is so much more than that, and correcting grammar is actually only one step, best done quite near the end of your process.

Below are the four main stages of feedback and editing you need to understand. You will likely do the first two (revising and structural editing) yourself, preferably with the aid of a professional developmental editor. The second two are best handed off to a fresh set of professional eyes.

1. Developmental Editing/Revising
Developmental editing is the process of taking a raw set of material and shaping it into a true manuscript that flows the way you envisioned and fulfills your purpose for the book.

A great developmental editor can hold the vision for your book and help you organize the material into a compelling narrative structure that fulfills it. They'll help you see what parts need to be brought forward and highlighted, where you have included excess that can be trimmed, and how to create a flow from start to finish that draws the reader along. This editor will be able to "hear" your voice through the chaos of the first draft and bring it out in a powerful way.

Developmental editors do not generally make many changes (if any) for you, but rather show you where changes can be made to make your draft more powerful. For most authors, the quality of their developmental editing strongly defines the quality of their finished product. See chapter fourteen for guidance on choosing your developmental editor.

Revising is the process the author undergoes after developmental editing.

Structural Editing

Structural editing shares a good deal with developmental editing, but focuses more tightly and on more detail. It is usually performed after the first draft has been revised into a full manuscript, following one or more rounds of developmental editing.

The structural edit focuses on how your manuscript is executed in terms of the ordering of the material and how it transitions from one section to another. This level of editing often happens at the chapter and paragraph level, helping you move material to where it can be most effective within the manuscript, and creating transitions to keep the reader moving through the book.

A structural editor may make some changes for you, but should always track the changes so that you can see what has been done and decide for yourself whether it makes your book better. They will likely also provide comments and suggestions for changes that you may want to make yourself.

Copyediting

Copyediting is what most people think of when they think of editing. Here, a professional grammarian will check your punctuation, spelling, syntax, and grammar. They'll help you clean up excess verbiage that doesn't contribute to your voice, and generally make the draft look great.

They will also create a "style guide," which will contain all the "rules" for how your voice is expressed in writing. For instance, if you capitalize nouns in a non-standard way as part of your style, that will be noted in your style guide. If you use ellipses in a particular way, that will be noted as well. If you swear a lot but fill in the vowels with asterisks…that goes in your style guide. If most of your book is following standard rules such as those in the Chicago Manual of Style, the name of the rule book that is used will be referenced in your style guide. The style guide helps ensure that your final manuscript is consistent, clean, and professionally presented, even in the ways in which you depart from the "standard" way of doing things.

Copyediting should always be provided by a professional who specializes in this level of detail work, who knows the standard rules in the main standard style guides, as well as how to document deviations from them. This should never be done by the same person who does your developmental and structural editing, as it's an entirely separate skill set and also requires fresh eyes.

Proofreading

Proofreading is the final step in preparing your manuscript for publication, usually after it has been formatted. It is a highly detailed, very precise final review to ensure your entire manuscript follows the style guide and is as clean and perfect as it can possibly be: Every punctuation mark where it needs to be, every word in place.

Proofreading should always be performed by someone who has not worked closely with the manuscript previously.

Exercise: Read On!

Your next task will be to choose a developmental editor, and for that, you need the contents of chapter fifteen.

YOUR DEVELOPMENTAL EDITOR
is a critical wayfinder through
this challenging terrain

In the publishing world, a developmental editor is a writing partner who reviews a rough draft and helps you form and fashion it into a respectable manuscript. The developmental editor isn't there to check your grammar and make sure all your sentences are perfectly coiffed. They're there to help your book live up to the vision you have for it.

The developmental editor should understand narrative and story and see the arc of what you need to create. They should deeply understand what you are trying to do, and know how to help you get there. They'll help you organize the material to flow the way it needs to and keep the reader's attention. They'll hear your "voice" through the noise of the messy first draft and help you truly claim it.

In short, they're the superheroes who can help you turn a messy draft into a fully executed manuscript.

Here's How to Choose Your Developmental Editor

Authors in my full program have me for developmental editing, so the process is seamless. I also offer developmental editing as a stand-alone for authors who just need a little help. Whether you work with me or want to look further afield, you'll want to closely evaluate anyone you hire. This role is too important to take lightly.

Here's what you want to see in a developmental editor:

First: They generally approve of you and your work

No Aunt Mildred's!

Second: They understand your work

If you're in my program, you're here because I already approve of your work and understand your vision. I wouldn't have accepted you into the program if I didn't. Done and done. Otherwise, you should expect your developmental editor to ask insightful questions and to reflect back to you a clear understanding of your goals and vision.

Uncle Dave, who loves you to the moon and back and thinks you're a big shot because you were in that local car dealership commercial that one time when you were a teenager, and tells everyone you still do "something to do with Hollywood," might make a great cheerleader for your work, but if he doesn't actually understand what you do, he won't be able to provide useful feedback that makes your draft better.

No Uncle Daves!

Third: They feel "safe" to you

Listen to your gut. If someone doesn't feel safe, they probably aren't. That doesn't mean they're necessarily abusive or bad, it just means that, for you, the relationship isn't safe for the feedback you want.

Trust yourself.

Fourth: They are highly qualified and you love their work

You absolutely should check your developmental editor's credentials to ensure you're working with a seasoned professional who knows what they're doing and can do it well. At minimum, you should feel that your editor:

- Has experience with your type of book
- Resonates with your work
- Understands what you're trying to accomplish with it
- Can see your vision and hold it in their hands
- Has deep expertise in storytelling, narrative structure, and voice

- Is capable of providing valuable feedback on how to shape your next draft
- Will provide that feedback in an actionable and useful manner
- Is a masterful storyteller in their own right
- Can see to the heart of what makes your story unique and valuable
- Will hear your voice through the noise and help you bring it out

Ask to see examples of their own work as well as that of authors they've helped. You may want to purchase a book or two from their list of titles. Ask if you can speak with authors they've worked with to find out what the experience was like for them.

When you find an editor who fulfills all of these criteria and whose work you admire, you're ready to rock and roll. Hand that baby off.

Storytime: The Developmental Editor's Perspective

When Delia delivered her beautiful first draft into my hands, I gasped with delight at her stunning voice. Also, she had followed my instructions well: Her draft was messy, gnarly, lengthy, and full of unnecessary material and long-winded stories that didn't serve the main narrative.

I adored it.

I cooed and ga-gaed over it.

Then I went to work on it.

I refreshed myself on her book foundation and dove headfirst into the work. Using my superpowers, I saw what was working and what wasn't. I saw the narrative arc that was wanting to emerge. I saw what needed to come out, and what needed to be enhanced. I saw the scintillating passage that wanted to become the introduction, and I saw the patterns that wanted to become themes throughout.

Most of all, I saw her voice and how beautiful it was, and how it needed to come to the forefront to draw the reader in and keep them reading.

After her two-week rest period, I delivered Delia's feedback to her. She received the original document with my extensive mark-ups, plus the developmental feedback brief that helps the author understand where to begin and how to focus their revision process. I delivered these assets via a video call to give her the overview and orient her to the materials. Then we scheduled a follow-up call for the following week to answer the questions she would certainly have as she worked through the draft again.

Like many authors, Delia worked hard to apply the feedback I provided. And like all the authors in our program, I guided her every step of the way.

And now, Delia has a book that her readers consistently say they can't put down.

How to Know a Developmental Editor is Right for You

1. They approve of you and your work, emphatically.
2. They understand your work.
3. They feel safe.
4. They have experience with your type of book.
5. They have deep expertise in storytelling, narrative structure, and voice.
6. They resonate with your work.
7. They understand what you're trying to accomplish.
8. They can hear your vision through the messiness of a first draft and hold it in their hands.
9. They provide valuable feedback on how to shape your draft to achieve your vision.
10. They provide that feedback in an actionable and useful manner.
11. They are a masterful storyteller in their own right.
12. They see to the heart of what makes your story unique and valuable, and can reflect that back to you.
13. They hear your voice through the noise and help you bring it out.

Exercise: Find Your Developmental Editor

If you don't already have someone lined up, this is your next task. Get out there and find your person!

REVISING is the hardest and most critical part of your process

I said this near the beginning, and it's time to repeat it again, this most unfortunate of news: Writing a first draft is hard, but the first round of revisions is harder. Brace yourself.

But there's good news, too. When you're done with this round, you will have crossed a major threshold that most writers, even those who write hundreds of thousands of words, never cross: You will have a legitimate manuscript.

At the end of your rest period, after your developmental editor has worked on your draft, you'll begin the transformation process from first draft to revised manuscript. Upon completion of your first round of revisions, your document will graduate from "draft" to "manuscript."

I make this distinction because "manuscript" implies a more formal completion, something close to a finished book. This can be a lot of pressure for that first draft, whose only job is to exist! But completing the first round of revisions makes your book feel more like a book and less like a word salad.

So. Now that your first draft is complete, you've taken a break, and you've received feedback from your developmental editor, you're ready to do the revisions that create the shift from draft to manuscript. Fancy, right?

At the start of your revision process, expect a call with your developmental editor to go over your feedback together. During this call, they should review the key points to focus on, and give you personalized instructions for moving forward. It's a good idea to have a second meeting about a week later, to address any questions that pop up for you while working with their feedback.

Your job is to take that feedback, and your own understanding of your vision, and use it to firm up the structure and flow of your manuscript.

Most authors find that this work requires them to work in longer chunks of time than the first draft did. For instance, if you've been working in one-hour segments, you may find 2-hour segments better for this part of the process. Some folks find it easiest to block out a whole day or two.

Longer chunks of time are helpful because you need to be able to hold the whole book in your head at once while you work on the revisions. It can take a while at each session to get it all in your head again, and then you need time to do the work.

A great developmental editor will make this part of the process easier on you by providing signposts and guides on where to focus your attention and time. But no matter how good your editor is, it's important to also hold on to your own inner knowing, and follow your own guidance. This is your book, your voice, and the only opinion that really matters at this point is yours.

Don't get bogged down right now by focusing on nitty gritty details. Focus on the big picture:

- Organizing your material
- Structuring the main narrative arc
- Deciding what to leave in and what to take out
- Choosing and/or developing a captivating opening
- Drafting and/or improving a satisfying closing
- Bringing forward your authentic voice

That's it. Don't get sidetracked. It may help you to review chapter's three's explanation of narrative structure. Then, take a deep breath, review your North Star Statement and the latest version of your working outline, and the feedback brief from your developmental editor. Then open up your draft and get started.

Step 1. Read through all the main feedback quickly

Inside your draft, your editor should have provided you with lots of comments and tracked changes. Review them quickly, keeping your eyes open for key points that feel especially important.

Step 2. Gut (and heart) check

Feedback is subjective. Not everything your editor says will make sense to you. Not even if it's me!

Remember that this is *your* book, so you can take and leave what works for you or doesn't. Don't let someone else's opinion of your book change what you know in your heart to be right for it.

Sometimes, the feedback you receive will resonate deeply with what you already know. Listen to that feedback!

Sometimes it will seem confusing. Check in with yourself and/or your editor to ensure you understood the feedback. If the feedback makes more sense and feels right to you after that, then use it. If you're still confused by it, ignore it.

Sometimes you may really hate the feedback. This is okay! It doesn't necessarily mean your editor messed up, or that you messed up. All it means is that feedback can be subjective, and you disagree.

If something does bother you, though, don't dismiss it right away. Assuming your editor is good and understands and values your work, it's worth spending a little time to parse why it troubles you.

- Is it because your editor doesn't understand what you're trying to do?
- Is it just plain wrong?
- Is there something in it that is helpful to you but the specific approach doesn't work for you?
- Are you trying to hide from something you know to be true?
- Are you reacting because it feels like an insult, and you're feeling defensive, but underneath you actually see the practicality of the suggestion?

Any answer to these questions is legitimate. Just sit with the questions until you know the answers, and then move forward accordingly.

You don't have to incorporate every piece of feedback.

You may also want to reach out to your editor and ask for more information or input in regard to suggestions that don't feel right to you. Perhaps they didn't communicate clearly what they meant, or perhaps you read it differently than they intended. Regardless, they should be able to help you gain clarity around what you want to do with it.

A great developmental editor will see the through-lines in your work and help you fashion a narrative structure that brings them to the front, while creating a flow that keeps your readers with you and makes your voice shine.

Jordan's first draft felt to him like a lot of random stories he'd dumped onto the page. But when we looked at his foundation statement, we saw that most of them made sense for what he was trying to do. I was able to "hear" the flow that the stories wanted to have in order to accomplish his vision. I showed him what needed to stay in, what needed to come out, and how to connect the stories to make a complete narrative. By the second draft, he was feeling good about what he'd accomplished and could see clearly how it was going to end up as the book he knew he wanted to write.

Step 3. Shape the Draft

Just as with your first draft, you can work with this next draft in any order that pleases you.

Start with the biggest changes and massage the overall draft into shape.

Or, start with some small comments so you can knock them out quickly and get to the big stuff later.

Or, start with something in particular that's calling you and feels fun.

Or, start with something that's nagging at you that you just want to get out of the way.

It's up to you, but remember: Don't get focused on nitty gritty details at this stage. If you're in one section making changes to your commas and periods, and then later you decide to remove that section, you'll have wasted a LOT of precious time. And it'll make it harder to make that difficult decision to remove the material, in the event that you need to.

This is your big-picture revision stage. Don't get mired in the weeds.

Where to Focus in Early Revision Round(s)

- Moving sections around so that the order makes more sense and the flow works
- Adding sections, especially in the beginnings and endings of the book and each chapter, to fill it out and add context
- Removing sections that don't work or are unnecessary
- Adding transitions to help the reader navigate from one section to the next
- Generally cleaning up the flow of the work

- Getting the order and structure of chapters & subsections more-or-less "right"
- Removing repetitive content

Where should you NOT focus your attention at this stage?

- Grammar
- Spelling
- Punctuation
- Making each paragraph shine in its finest glory
- Crafting sentences to perfection]

Step 4. Park Things in Your Parking Lot

"In writing, you must kill all your darlings." William Faulkner

One of the hardest things about early revisions is the cutting. Almost everyone has to take things OUT of the draft in order to turn it into a manuscript. You may find that you feel strongly attached to some of what you know needs to come out.

It may be a story you realllllyyyy wanted to tell. Or a few paragraphs that you feel just shine with your personality. Or a point that feels important to you but somehow it's not directly relevant to this particular book.

Cutting material like this can be painful.

It's okay that you feel this way. It's normal. And? It's important not to let your attachment to a small portion overrule your devotion to the whole.

So, what to do?

Don't despair. This isn't your only book! It's just your first!

So instead of deleting material that doesn't fit, paste it into your Parking Lot (see chapter eight).

Voilà, you now have the start of Book 2 and/or valuable extra material to serve as social media fodder, book launch quotes, or anything else you want to do with it. Now you can refocus on finishing Book 1, knowing that all these beautiful snippets are safely stowed away, out of the way, ready to shine another day.

You may also find that there are sections that feel like they belong, but ultimately, you're just not sure how they flow with the rest of the book. It's good to check in with your developmental editor on this, and be prepared to remove them or wait until the end to decide where they go.

If you just aren't sure where to put something in the book, but you know it does belong in the book, you can cut it and paste it at the bottom of the document in a smaller "short term parking lot" area. Then, when you're done with the rest of your revisions, you can revisit this section and figure out where each part goes–or if it's ready to be moved to long-term parking.

Step 5. Review Your Work

At some point, you'll have worked through the full draft and moved everything into position within it.

You'll have added sections, moved sections around, and taken sections out.

You'll have added transitions so that the draft flows neatly from one section to the next, guiding the reader all the way.

You'll have responded to (or chosen to ignore) all of the feedback, and massaged the draft into a state of flow. It won't be polished to perfection yet, but it will feel like it's more-or-less: COMPLETE.

At this point, take a few minutes to review your outline and update it (if you're using Google Docs or similar, you can use the built-in Table of Contents feature to update it automatically based on your section headings). If everything seems mostly in order, check against the "How Do I Know My Manuscript Is Complete" checklist and then... hand it back to your developmental editor! Wooooo-hooooo!!!

How Do I Know My Manuscript is Complete?

Part of the magic of actually writing your book is knowing when to stop writing your book. As you learned in writing your first draft, this can be harder than it seems.

As you work through your revision process, there will come a point when it's time to set it aside and hand it back to your editor. If you're not sure, ask yourself these four questions:

1. Are the sections of the draft in the order I want them?
2. Do they flow more-or-less smoothly from one section to the next?
3. Have I said most of what I want to say in this book?
4. Do I FEEL like it's ready to be edited?

If you can answer "yes" to three out of four, you're ready.]

Exercise: Revise Your Draft!

Time Estimate: 2-4 weeks

Block out at least two hours at a time, according to how you work best, and get to it! While this part can be pretty grueling, the good news is that with the right help, it usually goes faster than the initial draft round. Expect about two to four weeks of hard work and then: Ta-da. A manuscript you can be proud of!

Draft Vs Manuscript

To help distinguish the different stages of the writing process, I distinguish between a draft and a manuscript.

Draft: Each version of your book's content is a draft. But only some versions qualify as a manuscript. A first draft is often a messy, half-incoherent, somewhat chaotic conglomeration of words and stories that is the raw material that will become a manuscript. Some authors may nail the manuscript on the first try, but I don't recommend trying, as that's a recipe for never getting done. Most authors complete at least one rough draft before achieving the level of "manuscript."

Manuscript: A book-length draft that is coherent, mostly complete, and at least roughly resembles the likely final version of your book's contents. It doesn't have to be perfect in order to be a manuscript. It can be messy, repetitive, and unpolished and still be a manuscript. It just has to be in the right order, with most of the contents present, and coherent as a complete book.

All manuscripts are drafts, not all drafts are manuscripts. Graduation from "draft" to "manuscript" usually occurs at the end of the first round of revisions, and it's an even bigger deal than completing the first draft. Celebrate!]

REST STOP

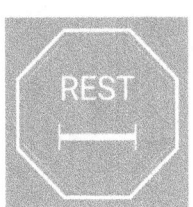

CHAPTER SEVENTEEN

EDITING brings your manuscript
all the way home

You may need several rounds of revision before you move into editing, and that's fine. Generally, each round is more granular than the one before, and at some point, you're ready to move into the editing stage, where you bring the manuscript all the way home.

Expect another call with your editor at this point, and another feedback brief with highlights, plus tracked edits within the draft. At this stage, the editorial feedback will likely be more granular than before. There may be big picture structural suggestions still, but it's likely to exist alongside tracked changes at the chapter and paragraph level, plus potentially some clean-up at the sentence level for your intro and conclusion.

Polish Like This

Most authors find this stage much easier to manage and can readily complete their edits in about an hour a day at their previous pace, in about two weeks or less.

Step One. Read through all the main feedback quickly.

Look for the key points that feel the most important and biggest. You should be able to find this in your feedback brief and during the call with your editor.

Step Two. Polish her up

For this round of editing, you will likely find it easiest to start at the beginning of your manuscript and work through it in order. You may find that printing it out to look at it on paper helps you visualize your work.

Step Three. Gut (and heart) check

Review each suggestion from your editor and check it against your own gut and heart. As always. YOUR book. YOUR way. Accept the changes that make sense to you, add sections and delete them where it feels right, and plug on through the manuscript till it's done.

At this point, it's okay to get a little bit into the weeds. You're moving toward completion, so you want to pay attention to details.

- Clean up your paragraphs
- Take out excess rambling
- Add transitions
- Perfect your stories
- Polish the intro and conclusion to near perfection

Work through the draft as many times as you need to get it pretty darn near the way you want it.

Step Four. But Don't Get Stuck

If you find yourself obsessing over one section, don't.

Just get the manuscript as good as you can get it for now, and don't worry if you're still finding extra words after you've been over it in detail.

It's okay.

Get it good enough and call it good enough.

You'll need a copyeditor to get it even closer to perfect. Everyone needs a great copyeditor. We'll address that in the next chapter.

Step Five. But Do Obsess About Your Intro and Conclusion

The first sentence of your book determines whether the reader will read the first paragraph. The first paragraph determines whether they will read the first page. The first page determines whether they will read the first chapter. And the first chapter determines whether they will read the book.

The ending of your book determines whether the reader recommends it to their friends.

I don't want to scare you, but these are the facts.

Of course it is a bit of an oversimplification, but the truth is: You cannot afford to flub on the start and the finish of your book.

One of the biggest tasks of the developmental editor is to help you unearth the part of your work that belongs at the beginning, and the clincher that helps you nail the ending. You need something that will connect with your reader immediately at the start, then you need it honed down to hit just exactly the right note in just exactly the right number of words. And at the end, you need something that sums up everything in the book, leaves your reader with a feeling of satisfaction, and tells them something they'll never forget.

When you've done that, the reader won't notice your hard work. They'll just keep reading and then recommend your book to all their friends.

Which is exactly what you want them to do.

There is an art and a science to understanding how the human story brain works, what matters to the specific target reader, and how the author's unique voice can best capture and hold attention with those readers.

A great developmental reader will help make the process of nailing this easier, less painful, and more effective. Regardless, you should expect to spend a substantial amount of your editing time toward the end of the process on these two things: The beginning and the ending.

And this latter part of your editing process is the time to be focused on this. Now you understand what's in your book, how it's structured, what stories you'll tell. Now you're ready to get the beginning and the ending right.

Obsess over it. K?

Polish it till it's so good your reader won't even notice it's good. They'll just know they want more.

Step Six. OMG YOU HAVE A COMPLETE MANUSCRIPT

When you are done with this round of edits, BE DONE.

Don't obsess.

Listen for that feeling in your heart and gut that says: This is complete.

And be complete.

Sit back. Breathe. Do a happy dance.

Grab a friend and go dancing. Grab a dog and go hiking. Grab a book and go sit at a coffee shop.

Take a break, and then come back to your computer and print the manuscript out. You need to hold it in your hands.

You need to FEEL that you are an author with a COMPLETE MANUSCRIPT.

And you need this for posterity, to have something solid to show your great-grandkids, to say, "This was the original. Before it was a published book, it was this."

Bind it with clips, or ribbon, or whatever pleases you. Put a cover sheet on the front with the title in bold letters and the subtitle below it. At the bottom of the cover page, put your byline:

By [Your Name Here]

There will be more rounds of edits, but your hardest writing work is done. The book is complete.

You are an author. You have a complete manuscript. Savor. This. Moment.

Be Prepared for The Crash, Too (I'm So Sorry)

Here's where I tell you some hard truths. Many authors at this stage experience a bit of a crash.

They've worked so hard for so long to bring this baby book into the world, and now it's done. And now what?

It can be a little like postpartum blues. You may feel:

- Elation followed by depression
- Sadness
- Numbness
- Exhaustion
- Confusion
- Shock

All of this is natural and normal, and nothing to be concerned about. But it is a good idea to set yourself up for support during this time. Talk to friends ahead of time to ask for whatever support will help you most. Go get a massage, drink some lovely tea, sleep late, watch movies till your eyes close at night.

Whatever it takes. Just be ready to support yourself and be supported through it. Don't worry, your book is okay. It's birthed. And now you can rest. There will be more to come, but for now, rest.

Finally, You're Almost–But Not Quite–Done

When your draft is polished, but before you hire a copyeditor, is the time for a few additional steps.

You may have been tempted all along to let friends and family read the amazing work you're doing. I hope you have resisted. Now that you are nearing the very end, you may begin to consider offering a sneak peek to a few select friends you know will cheerlead for you plus possibly a few folks in your target reader list who can let you know if you've missed anything important.

It's important to severely limit this still. Less is definitely more. You are the expert, so don't let anyone else's opinion send you sideways.

Then, finally, you're ready for the final three steps, which are covered in the next three chapters.

Exercise: Polish Your Manuscript

Time Estimate: 2-4 weeks

Use the steps in this chapter to get your manuscript into the shape you want it in. OMG YOU'RE ALMOST DONE.

How Do I Know When My Manuscript is Complete?

Before you hand your manuscript off to a copyeditor, you want it as close to perfect as you can get it, because once you've paid someone to go through it with a fine tooth comb, you don't want to make any further substantial changes.

Here are the questions to ask to know if you're really ready for the next step.

1. Are my introduction and conclusion really freaking good?
2. Does the middle flow the way I want it to?
3. Does the book say everything I want to say and nothing more, nothing less?
4. Does the manuscript feel reasonably "clean" and ready to be read by the people I want to reach?
5. Do I FEEL like it's complete?

If you can answer "yes" to four out of these five, then you're done. You have a complete manuscript, ready to begin the final stages of editing and publishing. WOW. You did it.

REST STOP

Chapter Eighteen

REQUEST FEEDBACK slowly, mindfully, intentionally, or not at all

A t some point in your writing process, you will begin to want to share your book with friends. This is totally normal and, in fact, *some* feedback from non-professionals can be very helpful. Just be careful. The wrong feedback can set you back, cause you to question yourself, send you down the wrong trail, or even cause you to lose hope and quit altogether.

Here are four guidelines for requesting and receiving feedback that will help you, instead of hurting you.

1. Never share too soon

First and foremost, never share your manuscript until it is nearly complete, except with a carefully chosen developmental editor who is accustomed to seeing drafts in an early, messy form (see chapter fifteen for tips on finding your developmental editor).

Protect your peace, and protect your vision.

Allowing someone else's ideas and feedback to interfere with what you know you need to do is like pouring poison on the ground where you've just planted a seed. Waiting until the book is close to complete will help ensure that your work is robust enough to survive examination.

2. Carefully vet anyone you decide to share with

Before you share your work with anyone, apply the same basic principles to them that you used to select a developmental editor: Don't share it with people who hate you. Don't share it with people who don't understand what you're doing. Don't share it with people who are not enthusiastic about your work.

Choose people who are members of your ideal audience, fellow professionals in your field, or are otherwise connected to your work in a meaningful way. Your coach may be a good choice, people you've worked with successfully in the past can be a good choice, and any trusted person in your professional network may be helpful, as long as they meet the "loves and understands your work and wants to help you" criteria.

3. Limit the number of people you share with

Too many cooks in the kitchen, etc., etc. Other than your professional editors, limit the number of people you share your manuscript with to between one and three. Seriously. I know that is a small number. I promise it is enough. More than that, and you will turn your head sideways and set yourself back by weeks or months.

Don't worry. When the book is out there, you will get plenty of broad feedback from a wider audience. Maybe they'll see things your carefully selected professional editors didn't and that were also missed by your carefully vetted feedback partners. Maybe? But even so, never fear. You can update the volume later.

But in the meantime, you actually have a complete book that is not stuck in an endless cycle of trying to please too many voices that are not *your* voice. And it's your voice that matters here.

4. Be explicit and detailed in your request

Never send a manuscript out for feedback without explicit instructions on what you are looking for. In order to do that, you must understand clearly what you are looking for. You already have a professional editor, right? So you don't necessarily need that level of feedback.

Provide readers with a list of questions that will actually help you. Here are some examples:

- Is there anything else you want to see in this book that isn't covered?
- Are there parts of the book that feel slow and sluggish to you?
- Are there parts of the book that stand out as especially interesting and powerful to you?
- Does anything feel unclear or in need of extrapolation?
- Do you notice any areas of repetition that could be streamlined?
- Are there specific stories you especially enjoyed?
- How does the book FEEL to you?
- What's your favorite part about it?
- What would make the book better?

You may also want to tell feedback partners the kind of feedback that you DON'T want. For instance:

- Spelling and grammar checks
- Disagreeing with concepts

Consider reminding them that their feedback is valued and valuable both for the things they love *and* the things they don't love. Tell them that it's okay not to read the whole thing: If they get bored partway through, that's actually valuable feedback in itself, because it tells you somewhere that you can pick up the pace to hold your readers' attention. Ask them to share with you where they stopped, so you can take a look at that section.

Give them a deadline for when you need to receive the feedback in order to incorporate it. Give them at least two weeks, but up to six is reasonable. Account for this in your timeline, and consider requesting feedback at the same time that your developmental editor is working on your final round of professional feedback.

And finally, let them know that you appreciate them no matter how much or how little feedback they're able to provide. Your relationships are at least as important as feedback!

One last note on feedback partners

It is also COMPLETELY ABSOLUTELY okay to NOT request feedback from non-professionals at all. You know your business. You know what needs to be said. You've hired professionals to help you get it all out. You are not required to "field test" your book before it goes out. Trust yourself and trust your professional partners.

To paraphrase a current (as of this writing) VP of the US, Kamala Harris: You know things. People need to know what you know. If the ship were sinking and you knew it, would you worry about how you look or whether people liked you? Or would you say what you know because it's important and people need to know it.

The ship is sinking. The world needs what you have to say. Trust that.

Exercise: Solicit Feedback (maybe)

Time Estimate: 30-45 minutes

Take a few minutes to make a list of people you might like to receive feedback from. Check the list against your criteria. If you end up with a list of more than three people, narrow it down to one each from different categories: Perhaps one who fits your ideal reader profile, one who knows your work as a colleague, and one who is a friend you deeply trust.

Send an email asking if they'd be willing to review your manuscript, along with the word count and timeline, so they can make an informed decision.

Then, write out a list of questions you'd like answered. What kind of feedback would be most helpful to you? How would you like them to interact with your draft? What do you NOT want them to say or share with you?

When you feel fully ready and your partners have agreed to the assignment, draft up an email with your questions and requests, make a separate copy of your manuscript for each person (label it with their name), and send it out to them.

CHAPTER NINETEEN

HARM REDUCTION keeps you
safe and your readers happy

Claiming your voice and birthing your book is a very, very brave thing to do.

Putting your work out there into the world is terrifying. And beautiful. And courageous. And amazing.

You want it to have the biggest, most beautiful, most positive impact it possibly can.

One common fear is that you may have said things in your manuscript that might cause harm to others–or cause them to harm you. This is a real fear, and a real danger. As for doctors, so for authors: First, do no harm.

This comes up for most authors very early in the process, the fear of doing harm. Maybe you have living family members who might get their feelings hurt. Maybe you don't want them to know everything you have to say. Maybe there are potential legal issues or concerns about people coming after you to harm you.

This is so common that it's nearly universal among the authors I work with. During the first draft phase, I encourage them not to worry about this, yet. Just get the words down, and we'll worry about harm reduction later. Anything that might cause harm can almost always be worked out and worked around in the last stages of manuscript production.

And now we're there. So let's talk about it.

Plagiarism, Libel, and Slander

Depending on the content of your book, you may be concerned about the potential for some of your work to be plagiarism—if, for instance, you were inspired by someone else's work, and you're not sure if you've given appropriate credit.

Or, you might be concerned about harm you might cause to people you love by sharing stories that might hurt them.

You may worry that something you say in your book might lead someone to accuse you of libel or slander.

Or, if you're an abuse survivor, you may worry that your abusers may track you down and use what you say against you, to harm you again.

These are all valid, important concerns. Here's how to address them.

When You're Concerned About Plagiarism

A great copyeditor can help you identify and address areas in your book that may fall afoul of copyright laws. It's always better to err on the side of caution. Cite your sources, remove excess quotation of others' work, and run the draft through a copyright or plagiarism screening program if you are concerned.

When You're Concerned About People You Love

When you have a concern about people you love, this is the time to speak to them. Tell them what you are doing and that your book contains portions that might affect them. Ask them to read the sections about them, and share those sections (selectively) with them if they agree to it.

Shannon spoke widely of people she knew in her autobiographical work *Bonnie Bodacious*. Rather than risk relationship harm, she sent copies of each section to the people they impacted ahead of time. In her case, every one of them loved every word, and most of them came to her book launch party later. This gave her enormous peace of mind and preserved the important relationships in her life.

I did the same thing with the chapter titled "Yes, Of Course" in my memoir *Remembering Our Way Home*. The named parties came back with a resounding YES: They loved what I'd written, even the part about one of them seeming "pompous," and were honored to be included.

You may or may not get the same reception. If someone you love has concerns, you can address them. You may take their portion out, edit it to address their concerns, or speak more generally without naming anyone, in order to protect their feelings. Have a conversation with them about what would feel best to them, and then work around their needs in the way that seems best to you and agreeable to them.

As with requesting more general feedback, be specific with your loved ones. Tell them exactly the kind of feedback you are asking for, as well as what you are not asking for.

When You're Concerned About People Hurting You

In other cases, you may be concerned about what will happen if you speak up about things that were done to you by people who are no longer in your life, or with whom you have a strained relationship.

First of all, just know that you have every right to speak up about things that were done to you. Your story is yours to tell. Sometimes, we make the decision that does the most good, even though it may have consequences that we don't enjoy.

"If people wanted you to write warmly about them, they should have behaved better." ~ Anne Lamott

However, that doesn't mean that doing so won't have consequences for you. You also absolutely have the right not to speak up if the costs outweigh the benefit for you.

Carefully consider the pros and cons of sharing, and decide whether you're willing to weather any potential consequences. You may choose to edit your work to reduce the possibility that the people you speak of will identify themselves or come after you, or you may to choose to speak out directly, depending on your circumstances and calling.

It's important to work closely with your developmental editor throughout the process to fashion the book in a way that doesn't expose you to undue harm.

If you're feeling a lot of emotional turmoil over these decisions, use Root 11 to work with those emotions, and consider seeking professional therapy to help you sort through them.

Additionally, you should be aware that in some cases what you say in print might be construed as libel or slander for legal purposes. Even if it isn't technically libel or slander, an offended party may sue you and cause trouble for you, even if they eventually lose the suit. Your copyeditor may be able to help you navigate these lines and in some cases it may be worthwhile to seek the assistance of an attorney to address legal concerns.

Diversity, Equity, and Inclusion

DEI, or Diversity, Equity, and Inclusion refers to the practice of reviewing systems, processes, and outputs to ensure that they are fair and equitable for all, including especially traditionally marginalized groups.

Any time we speak up, we have the potential to harm people unintentionally. This happens often when members of a privileged group are unaware of the impact their words and work can have on marginalized groups.

It is a mark of privilege that this harm is usually invisible to the people who cause it. For this reason, you may wish to invest in a DEI review of your manuscript before you send it out into the world.

A DEI review helps ensure that your book is as inclusive and representative as it can be based on who you are and who your readers are, and that it doesn't contain unintentionally harmful content.

Exercise: Reduce Harm

Time Estimate: 30-60 minutes

Take some time to consider who might be impacted by your book in ways that could cause harm. Consider people you know, people you used to know, and people you don't know who may be affected regardless. Make a plan to reduce harm to others as well as potential harm to yourself from any backlash you might receive by speaking out, and to manage any consequences that may occur for the ways you do choose to speak out.

CHAPTER TWENTY

A GREAT BOOK TITLE will do 80%
of your marketing for you

Whew. Here we are. You're almost done. Maybe you already have your book title nailed, but maybe you don't. Don't worry either way.

I put this section at the end of the book for one very simple reason: Because I don't know where else to put it.

In my years of working with authors, the timing of the discovery of a book title has been so varied that it's impossible to know when the "right moment" is going to strike.

Some people know the title of their book before they begin writing. Katrina Busselle's amazing *A Million Reasons Why You Can't* was named before she wrote the first word. And what a fabulous name it is!

On the other hand, I didn't have the name for this book until I was well into the 27th draft.

Some books are born out of the genius of a catchy title. Some books need to be written before the name becomes clear. Some books discover their name along the way.

For that reason, this chapter's location in this book is somewhat arbitrary. You'll get to it when you get to it.

But regardless of when you reach this step, there's no doubt:

Names matter.

The right name is the difference between an itchy sweater that you can't wait to get out of and a comfortable pair of cozy shoes you can't wait to step into and sit by the fire with.

Choosing a name for your book is at least as critical to your book as choosing a name for a child is for the child. And, unfortunately, there's no "most popular book names of the year" lists for you to peruse as you dream about the big day.

Also, unlike baby names, it's not okay if there are 10,000 other similar books of the same genre by the same name.

That simply won't do.

It must be unique to your category. Clear. Compelling.

It has to make people want to pick it up and read it.

It must reflect your personal brand.

It must reflect the contents of the book so that readers feel it has fulfilled its purpose when they are done.

It's a tall order.

It's hard work, naming a book.

For authors who get to the near the end of their process and still don't have a title for their book, I offer the following.

Step One: Relax into the process and don't force it.

Stress has a way of scaring away good ideas.

Step Two: Keep your mind and eyes and, especially, ears open for it.

It may show up when you least expect it. Stay tuned in.

Step Three: Allow your inner magic to guide you.

The name is already somewhere in you, you just have to let it come out.

Step Four: Talk to friends about your book.

Tell them what you're writing about at the moment. Notice the words you use. Notice when your friends light up with interest. Look for that "light up" moment and make a note of what you said that led to it. Your title may be buried in those sentences and phrases.

Step Five: Listen for what your friends repeat back to you and the questions they ask.

Your title may emerge from there. Write down interesting phrases and sentences to think about later. Compile your own personal "baby naming book" for your book.

Step Six: Look for phrases that pop up again and again.

As you work through each draft and have conversations with friends, **look for phrases that seem to pop up again and again** or that stand out to you in your manuscript. Are there themes emerging? Sentences that pop out of you that contain phrases that sound like titles? Your keys may be in those repetitions.

Step Seven: Pay attention to the titles and subtitles of books you love.

Develop an ear for their cadences and how they relate to the material of the books themselves. Let yourself be inspired by them. Add them to a section of your "baby naming book" called "book titles I love."

Step Eight: Study the Rules of Great Book Titles

Your book title has to stand out from every other book title in the world. But that doesn't mean there aren't guidelines that can help you nail your best title. Follow them or break them, knowing them will help you get there.

- The main title should (usually) be one to three words and no more than five.
- A subtitle can help clear up anything left uncertain in the title.
- It must be eye-catching and ear-catching.
- Hey, it better be something you are proud to live with for the rest of your life.
- It should be different from anything else in your genre.

It's critically important that you compare your choices to what's already in the market. You don't want your book competing with a massively popular book of the same title, or a book of the same title on a topic that is anathema to your purpose.

EXERCISE: NAME YOUR BOOK!

Time Estimate: 5 minutes to 12 years (sorry)

I'm kinda kidding about the 12 years, but it is true that you can't be sure how long this will take. At some point late in your process, if the title hasn't already emerged, block out some time for this work and use the steps in this chapter to guide you.

CHAPTER TWENTY-ONE

THESE PROFESSIONALS are indispensable to a polished, publication-ready manuscript

Now that you have a completed manuscript that you're proud of with a title you're excited about, and you're confident in your harm reduction, it's time to seek out the professionals who can help you get it from perfect to published.

Up to this point, hopefully you've had an incredible developmental editor guiding you, and perhaps a full-fledged book midwife and other helpers. Now it's time to bring in a whole new category of professional.

You and your team have had your eyes on the manuscript so many times, you can easily overlook simple things that need to be addressed. So it's critical to bring in fresh eyes.

At minimum, you will need:

- **A copyeditor.** Your copyeditor will go through the manuscript with a fine-tooth comb and help you make it look and feel professional.
- **A proofreader.** Your proofreader will read the final final FINAL draft of your manuscript after it has been formatted, to ensure there are no typos, grammatical errors, or other mistakes that would compromise the professionalism of your draft.

If you are publishing through traditional publishers, these professionals will be part of the team your publisher provides. If you are publishing yourself, you will need to bring them in yourself.

Additionally, if publishing yourself, you will need help with:

- Formatting the book
- Creating cover art
- Purchasing ISBNs
- Uploading the book to Ingram Spark and other platforms for publication

As with hiring a developmental editor, you should seek out references from people you trust, interview your candidates, vet them carefully, and then trust your gut. If you're working with a book midwife like me, your book midwife can likely help refer you to great candidates for many of these services.

EXERCISE: CHOOSE YOUR PROFESSIONALS

Time Estimate: 2-5 hours

If you're going it alone, it's time to take some time and seek out the professionals you'll need for the next stage of your journey. Whew, you're almost there. When you've found your copyeditor, take a deep breath, and hand off that manuscript!

REST STOP

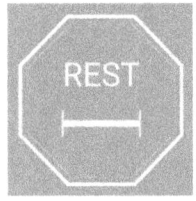

CLAIM YOUR VOICE
And light up the world

D ear reader, in this volume, I have given you everything I know to set you on the path to completing your
manuscript.

If there is anything left, it is only this, a reminder: I
believe in you.

When I saw that vision in the stars, the sky lit up so
bright like pinpricks in the fabric of the universe, so many
stars there were no dark patches left to hide the brilliance
from my eyes–I saw you there.

The mere fact that you want to write a book is evidence
that you have been called. The universe does not give us
longings without reason. If you are called, it is because
there is a need, and only you can answer your call.

There are infinite intelligences in the universe, and not one of them is yours, except you. We are each gifted with a special spark of madness that is our unique treasure to give.

> "You're only given a little spark of madness. You mustn't lose it."
> ~ Robin Williams

The fact that you have picked up this book is evidence that your unique voice is ready to be heard. Your gift is ready to be given. Your book is ready to be born.

Your soul is yearning to join the ranks of the stars and stretch out its tendrils to touch the others, that we all may live bigger and better and more beautifully in its light.

I believe in you because I believe in a brighter future for us all.

So, what are you waiting for?

Your call has come. Will you answer it?

Acknowledgments

There are many voices that rise through me in this little volume. I am grateful to every one of them.

There's Ken, who knew from the first words he read in that freshman essay in 1991 that I was the one he'd been waiting for. Ken, who believed in me before he even met me, who taught me everything he knew how to teach me, which was a lot, and inspired me to become everything I could be. Who woke within me my own voice.

Ken, who walks with me now from the other side of the veil. I miss you. I wish you were here to see this.

And there's my children, who inspire me every day with their humor and their wisdom and their insight, for whom I set myself free and through whom I learned to choose myself and claim my voice.

All the business owners and entrepreneurs and leaders at whose feet I earned my vicarious MBAs, who generously shared their expertise and advice and stories, who were guiding lights to me in claiming my own journey through the entrepreneurial wilderness.

Jessica Kantrowitz, whose steady hand and keen eye as a copyeditor has made this manuscript clean and polished and so much better than it would have been without her. Any errors remaining are my own.

Melanie, and Cathy, and Loye, my steady creative companions, accepting both my daily "this is what happened today" dumps and my inspired, "omg I just had the best idea" moments, and encouraging me through all of them.

All those who, through the harms they caused me, taught me how to walk away and how to heal. Whose cages served to prove how strong I am, how capable of setting myself free.

All the people I have never met but from whose wells I have drunk because they put their words out into the world as books and posts and essays and speeches, whose insights I have consumed and made a part of myself. There are too many to name, but especially Anne Lamott and Julia Cameron and Anne Rice and Stephen King and Robert McKee and Robin Wall Kimmerer and Jamie Sams and (I am an absorption of every word I have ever read) so many more.

The sun by whose light most of this was written and the moon whose glow carries me through the night, the stars and of course the earth who gives us all good things. The grass in which I cool my feet and the stones that shelter all the little creatures in the streams that inspire me. The water that gives us all life and has a life and intelligence of its own. The microbes that live in my body, converting food to fuel and a million other jobs I cannot do alone and could not live without. Each little electron that together with all the others becomes the electricity that fuels the tablet on which I am typing these words.

We are not alone, though most of us are asleep to just how much intelligence and love is available to us and offered up freely by everything around us.

Most of all I thank those regal, peaceful, deeply rooted beings whose teachings, companionship, and love have most directly impacted this particular work and my life as a whole: The trees. Especially, my particular friend Breathneach. Thank you for teaching me to breathe, to slow down, to be gentle with myself and others. Thank you for your steady, watchful, wise, and loving presence in my life, which has carried me through my hardest times and celebrated with me through my happiest. Thank you for your messages that always give me exactly what I need in each moment.

Thank you also to the fungal allies who connect us and whose visions live in these pages and in the tissues of my heart.

Gratitude also to the plants whose lives and work give us the paper on which this book is printed. All the beings who contribute to the ink with which the letters are made visible.

And my animal companions: Ace, my sweet golden-haired silly boy, who never leaves my side if he can help it. Your sense of humor and your constant, loyal, unwavering companionship have seen me through my darkest hours. Thank you for rescuing me. Thank you for reminding me to take a break and go for a walk.

Rigel, for exquisite kitty make-out sessions and making my colleagues and clients laugh, and for telling me when it's time to quit for the day. And magnificent Bella, for teaching me how self-ownership and love can co-exist. And Toby, though a newcomer to the household as of this final edit on this book, your freight-train-engine rumble of a purr has carried me through many a dark night.

My land. My ancestors. Grandmother Misty Mountain. Grandma Syble, whose love and adoration I needed like the seedling needs the sun. Great Mystery, Nkulukulu, the universe, Big Bang, Great Ancestor, All That Is, God–by whatever names we give you, any one of which is vastly inadequate–thank you for being, that we may all be.

My dragon kin. I feel you here with me.

My friends on Facebook. Yes, you're real. You matter to me, even those I've never met in person. This book is for you as much as for anyone else, and I thank you for coming along on this wild ride all these years.

To the authors I've worked with, who inspired this book most directly, and who inspire me every day with the light you bring to the world. I can't believe I get to do this work, to be behind the scenes watching you birth *your* work into the world. Watching your own voice emerge and pour out of you and become bigger and bolder and more powerful than you dreamed it could be. What an immense honor it is to work with you. Thank you, from the bottom of my heart. More than anyone else, this book is for you.

All these voices and more prove every day that no one voice exists alone, yet every voice is necessary to the well-being of the whole. And so, dear reader, may you also bring out the voice that is yours, that the world is longing to hear.

Dear reader, thank you. For taking this courageous step, for opening this book, for clasping my outstretched hand and choosing to accept the gift I hold in it. May our mycorrhizal threads be forever connected and may our connection awaken within us all that we can be.

About The Author

FEN DRUADÌN (they/them) is a prolific Appalachian author of several books including *Claim Your Voice*, *Remembering Our Way Home*, and *Morning After The Road Trip*. As a book midwife, Fen has helped dozens of authors go from crying in their coffee to producing a compelling manuscript they're proud to share with the world. A lifelong student of stories, Fen started reading before they could walk, and started writing before they can remember. They published their first local newspaper article at age 14, and never lost the bug to see their stories in print. They hold a degree in English literature from Huntingdon College and studied Greek and Latin classics at the University of Iowa. Over the course of a twenty-year career as a freelance writer, Fen produced thousands of articles, blogs, and long-form content pieces, many of them award-winning, including for local and national magazines, multi-billion-dollar companies like Autodesk, and international firms like Membrain.

Before moving into the work of helping authors write their own books, Fen ghost wrote several books for founders, CEOs, and philanthropists. Fen has dedicated a lifetime to understanding the structure, meaning, and impact of stories from ancient times to the modern day, across nearly every aspect of human life and in almost every context, from corporate to literary to practical to popular fiction. Fen integrates this background with a deep connection with the natural world and wilds of their home in Southern Appalachia plus an extensive study of psychology, brain science, systems thinking, myths and myth-making, shadow work, somatics, metaphysics, indigenous teachings, meditation, and multiple energetic and spiritual modalities, to create simple structures that effect deep transformation. Fen's work enables clients to claim their authentic voice and accomplish more than they ever dreamed. Learn more about Fen at fendruadin.com.